Message for the

MILLENNIUM

D0550103

Message for the
MILLENNIUM

Forty days at the feet of Jesus the Teacher

David WINTER

The Bible Reading Fellowship
OPENING THE BIBLE

Text copyright © David Winter 1998

The author asserts the moral right to be identified as the
author of this book.

Published by
The Bible Reading Fellowship
Peter's Way, Sandy Lane West
Oxford OX4 5HG
ISBN 1 84101 032 4

First edition 1998
10 9 8 7 6 5 4 3 2 1 0

Acknowledgments
The New Revised Standard Version of the Bible (NRSV)
copyright © 1989 by the Division of Christian Education
of the National Council of the Churches of Christ in the
USA.

The Holy Bible, New International Version, copyright ©
1973, 1978, 1984 by International Bible Society.

A catalogue record for this book is available from the
British Library

Printed and bound in Great Britain by Caledonian Book
Manufacturing International, Glasgow

This book explores and reflects on the teaching of Jesus as we find it in the Gospels. There can surely be no better way to celebrate the profound impact of that teaching on the human race over the past 2000 years than to examine it afresh. And there can be no better way to spend the last Lent of the second millennium than by engaging with the ideas of the man from whose birth we date our calendar—*anno Domini*—'in the year of the Lord'.

Many people who know the stories of the miracles of Jesus, and of his death and resurrection, are nevertheless largely ignorant of what he actually taught. So the wisdom and challenge of his ethical, moral and spiritual teaching are lost, even to many of those who claim to be his closest followers.

This book presents those teachings in the form of forty daily readings, with explanatory background and reflective material designed to make them accessible to the modern reader. But it is based on the teachings of Jesus, not the author's 'explanations'!

Although the material is arranged under forty headings, the book did not start with a list of topics for which I then tried to find relevant passages from the Gospels. In fact, the procedure was precisely the reverse. I went through the whole of the three 'synoptic' Gospels (Matthew, Mark and Luke—so called because they tell the story through the same 'eye'), noting every part of the teaching of Jesus as it occurred and 'filing' it under categories. From an examination of those categories I was able to assemble what I believe is a balanced and objective analysis of the teaching of Jesus, based entirely on the priorities which the Gospel writers themselves gave to each subject. For instance, there was surprisingly little, for a modern reader, about 'sex' in the teaching of Jesus, but a great deal about 'hypocrisy'. That's not my opinion, but a straightforward analysis of the weight of the evidence. So I hope that I have not only set out the core of the teaching of Jesus, but also managed to give it the emphasis and balance that he did.

I confined myself to Matthew, Mark and Luke not because I would wish in any way to detract from the value and authority of the magnificent Gospel of John, but simply because most of the actual teaching of Jesus is to be found in the first three Gospels. Where an insight from John's Gospel helps to illuminate a point in the synoptic accounts, I have not hesitated to introduce it. This is especially true, of course, when considering the teaching of Jesus about his own identity and purpose, which are among the great themes of the fourth Gospel. And for the Sundays, which are marked by a 'Pause for Prayer', the readings (based on the Revised Common Lectionary) are predominantly from John.

No teaching in history has more profoundly influenced the human race than the words of Jesus of Nazareth, a man who never wrote a book and had no formal status as a religious teacher. It is teaching to inspire and challenge. It turned the Roman Empire upside-down, and it's been turning people and societies upside-down ever since.

David Winter

CONTENTS

Fourth Week in Lent

Fifth Week in Lent

Holy Week

Material for Group Discussion

INTRODUCTION: JESUS THE TEACHER

As this is a book about the teaching of Jesus, it seems reasonable, before we begin to look at it, to ask whether we really have the teaching of Jesus as he originally gave it. Surely, people ask, his actual spoken words have got lost in the process of transmission? After all, there were no tape-recorders in ancient Galilee and Judea, with which to make a permanent archive of his sayings. So we are presumably relying on the memories of people who heard him, and passed on what he said to others, until—some forty years later, probably—the Gospels began to be compiled and those words were finally written down. To the modern person, whose memory depends on written (and now computerized) records, this lengthy gap seems to offer endless opportunity for distortion of the message.

A further difficulty, for those who know the New Testament, is the striking difference between the first three Gospels and the fourth. Matthew, Mark and Luke have a great deal of material in common, and for long stretches are word for word identical. John's Gospel, on the other hand, while clearly telling the same 'story', uses very different language. Indeed, John's Jesus *sounds* quite different from the blunt, down-to-earth rabbi of the synoptic Gospels. The reader may well ask which is the 'real' Jesus. Is it the mystic philosopher of John, or the homely preacher of Matthew, Mark and Luke?

The first answer to that is that it is a loaded question! The 'homely preacher' is nowhere near as 'simple' as he seems at first hearing, and the 'mystic philosopher' can be very down-to-earth when dealing with actual individuals. And there are times, as we shall see in these studies, when the Jesus of the synoptic Gospels speaks with a very Johannine voice! Nevertheless, there is a problem raised by both of these questions (the distorted transmission, and the differences between John and the other Gospels). It is one that can be resolved only by asking what the purpose of the Gospels is.

One obvious answer is that they are there to tell the story of Jesus: what he did, what he said and who he was. They don't do it in quite the style of a modern biography, nor do they pretend to be written by detached, impartial observers. The Gospels are written by committed people, people who have come to believe that Jesus of Nazareth was the promised Messiah and the Son of the living God, one who died and rose again—the saviour of the world. If they believe that, it's hard to expect them to be coolly objective! At the same time, these were honest men, and what they wanted to convey through their Gospels was the essential truth of the 'good news'. Each of the synoptic writers had a slightly different agenda and each went about his work in a slightly different way, using the same core material but shaping it to emphasize this or that aspect of the meaning of Jesus. John, too, had an objective, and that seems to have been to relate the Jesus of faith—Jesus as the early Christians had come to understand him—to the Jesus of Galilee and Jerusalem, someone the writer had known personally and whose impact he is now recollecting, perhaps long after the event.

So we have, in Matthew, Mark and Luke, three treatments of the same core material. That is obvious even to the casual reader. But where did that 'core material' come from? It seems strange to the modern reader that three compilers, probably working in completely different centres of the early Church—possibly Rome, Ephesus and Jerusalem—should have had so much material in common, unless it came from a common source. Some experts think that that source was an early (but now lost) written record, which they call 'Q' (for *Quelle*, German for 'source'). Others think that they were drawing on an oral record, the sayings and stories of Jesus recollected and recited from memory by the early Christian believers. In a largely oral age, memorizing things was far more important, and they were much better at it than we are. Without the advantage of a printed Gospel on the bedside table, they had to rely on their own memory of the vital 'teachings' of the Lord, which they had learnt by heart.

If that is so, it's a testimony to the accuracy of their memorizing that compilers working in different centres, hundreds of miles apart, could end up with great chunks of identical material. Whether they had recourse to an early written source, or simply to the sayings and stories memorized by the early Church—or to both—I think we can safely assume that Matthew, Mark and Luke are giving us the authentic sound and content of the teaching of Jesus, based on those sources. In other words, yes, we do have something we can properly describe as 'the teaching of Jesus'. Frankly, that teaching was just too important to those first believers to be treated lightly.

What were the distinctive marks of the teaching style of Jesus? The simplest answer to that question is that they were Jewish! One cannot read the Gospels without being struck again and again by how 'Jewish' it all is. The endless recourse to question and answer, the answering of one question with another one, the use of story and parable, of humour and irony: these have always been, and still are, the hallmarks of Jewish teaching. And they are all constantly present in the teaching of Jesus. No wonder the crowds called him 'Rabbi'— 'Teacher'—and that his followers were his 'disciples', learners who hung on his words, absorbed them, reflected on them, asked questions about them and tried to work out their deepest significance.

This is especially true of the so-called 'parables', the stories told by Jesus that had more than one level of meaning. Sometimes people say that Jesus told stories to make his meaning clear, but that is only partly true. In fact, at another level he told stories to make his meaning elusive, requiring his hearers to work at it, exercise faith and show spiritual insight in order to grasp the truth: 'Let anyone with ears to hear listen!' Indeed, in the same breath he told his disciples that he spoke to the crowds in parables so that they may 'look but not perceive, listen but not understand' (see Mark 4:9–12). For his disciples, the parables were unpacked by Jesus himself. For those he described as 'outside the kingdom of God' it was a more costly process, involving the use of the inward 'ear' of faith that alone can 'hear' the deepest truths.

Two other elements of the teaching style of Jesus are important if we are to grasp that 'deep truth'. One is his use of irony. Several times one suspects that something Jesus said is intended to be understood in an ironic way. His comment about the camel and the eye of a needle may be in that category, and—more obviously—the picture of the man with a plank in his eye trying to get a splinter out of his friend's. To speak of the Pharisees in their religious zeal 'straining out a gnat and swallowing a camel' is a marvellously inventive use of irony. Without a video record we can never be sure whether a saying of Jesus was accompanied by a smile or a wry grin, but I suspect that his commendation of the 'unjust steward' who cooked the books in order to ensure financial survival after his redundancy also falls into the same category (see Luke 16:1–9).

The other very typical device used by Jesus is hyperbole, the figure of speech in which a point is made, or emphasized, by a dramatic overstating of the case. In modern English idiom, for instance, we say 'everybody knows' when plainly everybody doesn't, or claim to be 'dying for a cup of tea' when in truth we are just a bit thirsty. Jesus uses this device a great deal in the Sermon on the Mount, as we shall see. If we make the mistake of taking him too literally, we might end up mutilating ourselves in order to avoid temptation, which seems an unlikely interpretation of his words (see Matthew 5:29). But the device makes the point in a memorable and arresting way.

One other thing must be added about the teaching 'style' of Jesus. The most frequently recorded judgment of his hearers was that he spoke 'with authority', and 'not as the scribes' (see, for example, Mark 1:22, 27). That doesn't mean, as it well might in modern English usage, that he was a dominating, assertive speaker, 'laying down the law' as we might say. That may well describe his teaching in some circumstances, but 'with authority' means much more than that. The word used for 'authority' (*exousia*) speaks of a *source* of authority, not a method of presentation. Jesus spoke on his own authority, not, as the scribes did, as a secondary interpreter of an already existing one. In other words—and this was the cause of public wonder—he spoke with the voice of God, the ultimate source of all authority. So 'they were astounded at his teaching, for he taught them as one *having* authority, and not as the scribes'.

His mission and his message

It seems that the teaching of Jesus as the synoptic Gospels record it changed quite radically at about the time of his 'transfiguration' (Mark 9, for instance). Until that point he had ministered to the crowds, healing the sick, teaching and preaching the good news of the kingdom. During this period he gathered together the inner core of his disciples, usually known as 'the Twelve' and later, with the sad exception of Judas Iscariot, to become his 'apostles'.

While walking with them in the north of the country, at Caesarea Philippi, he asked them first what the popular belief about him was. They suggested various ideas—that he was Elijah returned from heaven, or Jeremiah, or one of the other prophets. 'But who do *you* say that I am?' he asked. Peter, speaking for them all, replied, 'You are the Messiah.' In that single confession, the first phase of the teaching of Jesus was complete. Their confession was 'confirmed', so to speak, in the event of the transfiguration, when Jesus stood before them suddenly illuminated with the glory of heaven and accompanied, in a vision the three disciples present could never forget, by the figures of Moses and Elijah.

Now that they knew that great truth, revealed to them not by 'flesh and blood' but by his 'heavenly Father' (Matthew 16:17), they were ready for the next stage. It began disturbingly quickly, so disturbingly that Peter was minded to reject the idea completely, and earned a very stern rebuke for his pains. The trouble was that whereas, until then, the journey with Jesus had been one of joy and rich blessing, now, he warned them, it was to become a pathway to pain and suffering. 'The Son of man must suffer, and be delivered into the hands of wicked men, and crucified…' Suddenly there was a new and sombre note in the teaching of Jesus. They had recognized him as Messiah, and that was good. But now they had to learn the hard lesson that his messiahship was going to be on the model of Isaiah's suffering servant, rather than the triumphant warrior-king of earlier Jewish thought. The crowds tend to fade into the background in these final months, as the disciples themselves struggle with the meaning of these strange and in many ways unattractive new ideas.

Was the teaching of Jesus 'original'?

Until recent times it was generally assumed that the teaching of Jesus was wholly 'original', in the sense that no one was saying things like this, or using this kind of language, at the time. We now know, largely from the Dead Sea scrolls, that some of the apparently distinctive language and themes of Jesus were part of a new-style radical tradition which had grown up inside Judaism. For instance, the phrase 'the kingdom of heaven', which is so central to the teaching of Jesus, is an idea also found in the teachings of the Essenes, whose community in the Dead Sea area was a centre of religious and national renewal and revival at the time of Christ. We also find some similarities between the eschatological language of Jesus (dealing with the 'last things', judgment and the Day of the Lord) and that of the Essenes. They also share the conviction that the temple hierarchy and its systems had become corrupt—beliefs also held by John the Baptist, it seems.

None of this should surprise us. It is no contradiction of the divinity of Jesus to say that he was also truly and fully human, a person of his own time. After all, he spoke the language of his own people, Aramaic, and for all we know may not have been fluent in Greek or known any Latin at all. Being the Son of God wasn't a short cut to special knowledge of language. At the same time, while Jesus undoubtedly used ideas, themes and phrases from the religious world of his time, it would be true to say that he used them with an intensity, a particularity and at a depth of meaning that went far beyond the teaching of the Essenes, or other contemporary religious movements.

Unlike their teachings, the teaching of Jesus has universal application. Its survival and relevance two millennia later is proof of that. While much of the current religious debate of his time was narrowly nationalistic, his horizon was the whole of humankind. He came, it is true, 'for the lost sheep of the house of Israel', but he touched Romans and Syrians and Samaritans as well. His teaching was not motivated by sectarian interests or xenophobia, as much of the contemporary 'revivalist' cause was. He was driven by love—love of God, love of neighbour, love of enemy. He stands for all time as the master welcomer, his time and attention given to all who came to him, without distinction, truly 'a man for others'. He spoke not of rejection, but of acceptance.

His key words and phrases were kingdom of heaven, righteousness, obedience to God, 'being perfect'. He set before his hearers the priorities of the spiritual over the material, of the eternal over the temporal. Giving himself tirelessly for others, he called his followers also to a life of self-giving service. All of these ideas run like golden threads through the examples of his teaching in this book. It is not so much 'relevant' to the modern world (as we are frequently told it has to be if modern people are to respond to it) as *timeless*. The truths that Jesus taught 'relate' to our situation, to contemporary problems of attitude, behaviour, decision-making—of course they do. But they 'relate' because they are truth from 'beyond', eternal truth now earthed in human experience. The words of Jesus, as Peter once said, are 'words of eternal life' (John 6:68).

Yet in the end, one has to say that Jesus is more, much more, than what he said. Who he was and what he did are even more crucial to understanding his impact. His teaching, wonderful as it is even in cold print, has to be read in the light of his total 'mission', his calling to be the suffering servant of the Lord, the redeemer who gives himself for many—and who carries his principle of love to its final apotheosis on the cross. He is the great Giver, whose greatest gift was his own life offered for God's lost children.

If you live like that, you can teach like this.

The BEGINNING

of LENT

Day 1 (Ash Wednesday)

Ambition & Work

LUKE 12:16–21

> *Then he told them a parable: 'The land of a rich man produced abundantly. And he thought to himself, "What should I do, for I have no place to store my crops?" Then he said, "I will do this: I will pull down my barns and build larger ones, and there I will store all my grain and my goods. And I will say to my soul, Soul, you have ample goods laid up for many years; relax, eat, drink, be merry." But God said to him, "You fool! This very night your life is being demanded of you. And the things you have prepared, whose will they be?" So it is with those who store up treasures for themselves but are not rich toward God.'*

I suppose it's true that no one said on his deathbed, 'I wish I'd spent more time at the office.' On the other hand, the daily pressure to succeed—or, for that matter, to deliver the daily bread—is enough to keep most of our noses to the grindstone for much of our lives. And there is in every human being a need for 'success', to feel that we're good at *something*. For many people, that need is either fulfilled or frustrated in the area of our daily work.

'Ambition' is a strange concept, and it embraces many areas of life other than that of our 'job'. That human need to succeed can also express itself in sport, or amateur dramatics, or even the church. Disciplined and controlled, ambition can give us wings; but out of control, it can put us in chains. Think of poor Macbeth, desperate to be king and possessing many of the qualities that would qualify him for it—but brought down, in the end, by uncontrollable ambition. Many an otherwise admirable life has been destroyed by the desperate desire to succeed: to make a million, or get to be managing director, or achieve fame and fortune on the stage or the screen. The Bible has plenty to say about the virtue of hard work, and Jesus specifically commends those who make the most of their talents (see Matthew 25:14–30). But there are scathing words for those who allow the goals of money or power to take charge of their lives.

This memorable parable is a vivid example. Jesus envisages a man who is already rich, indeed so rich that he has nowhere large enough to store his crops. Instead, he 'goes for growth'. He sets in hand a plan to enlarge his barns so that they can hold enough grain to ensure him (and his family?) an affluent retirement in due course. (We may speculate whether a man like him would ever have retired, but that's another question!)

He then addresses his 'soul'—*psyche* is the Greek word, his 'inner self'—in terms of utter self-confidence. His plans are laid. Everything is mapped out. The expansion policy is in place. After that—it's always 'after that'—he will begin to take it easy and enjoy the fruits of his success.

But the story doesn't have a happy ending. God comments, as it were, from the wings. 'What a fool this man is! Doesn't he know that this very night his life is to end?' And God then puts the question which must always hang over human ambition and success: 'And the things you have prepared, whose will they be?' They are, after all, only 'things', valuable in this life, true, but of no value at all in the kingdom of heaven. It is not only a sharp warning about the perils of ambition and success—of the misuse of the God-given gift of work—but a powerful reminder about our priorities.

Once our priorities are right, then work and ambition can be 'baptized'. They can be used for the glory of God, as a celebration of his gifts and as a means of blessing to others. That seems to be the message of the parable of the sower (Matthew 13:1–12), where the hard work of the farmer and God's gift of the 'good seed' combine to produce rich blessing in the lives of many people. It's also, in a different way, the message of the apparently sharp words of Jesus to his disciples James and John, who came to him with an ambitious scheme to advance their careers in the apostolic 'team' (Mark 10:35–45). Mind you, Matthew tells us that it was their mother who came to Jesus, ambitious for her sons—a warning for those of us who, perhaps having failed ourselves, try to achieve success through our children! Jesus told the two disciples that it was the 'Gentiles' (the heathen) who set out to 'lord it' over people, to have power and status. *'But it is not so among you.'* Among the followers of the one who 'came not to be served, but to serve' (Mark 10:45), there is no room for pride of place, or love of power, or pursuit of riches for their own sake.

To REFLECT

I should work well, not for my bank balance or my reputation, but because God expects it of me. I should long to succeed, but above all in setting aside 'treasure in heaven'. I should want to use the gifts God has given me to the full, but primarily for his glory.

Other passages you may wish to consult: Matthew 13:1–12; Matthew 20:1–15; Luke 10:38–42; Matthew 25:14–30

ANXIETY

LUKE 12:22−32

He said to his disciples, 'Therefore I tell you, do not worry about
your life, what you will eat, or about your body, what you will wear.
For life is more than food, and the body more than clothing.
Consider the ravens: they neither sow nor reap, they have neither
storehouse nor barn, and yet God feeds them. Of how much more
value are you than the birds! And can any of you by worrying add
a single hour to your span of life? If then you are not able to do so
small a thing as that, why do you worry about the rest? Consider
the lilies, how they grow: they neither toil nor spin; yet I tell you,
even Solomon in all his glory was not clothed like one of these. But
if God so clothes the grass of the field, which is alive today and
tomorrow is thrown into the oven, how much more will he clothe
you—you of little faith! And do not keep striving for what you are
to eat and what you are to drink, and do not keep worrying. For it
is the nations of the world that strive after all these things, and
your Father knows that you need them. Instead, strive for his
kingdom, and these things will be given to you as well. Do not be
afraid, little flock, for it is your Father's good pleasure to give you
the kingdom.'

Here is a splendid example of the contrast that Jesus constantly draws
between the 'nations of the world' and the 'people of the kingdom'.
The 'nations'—the word is *ethnoi* in Greek, from which we get our
word 'ethnic'—are the pagans, those without God's law, those who
are as yet strangers to his covenant. Not surprisingly, then, their goals
are earthly and their ambitions limited to survival and physical well-
being. Over against them are the 'people of the kingdom', the 'little
flock'—generally, I suppose, the people of Israel, but here specifically
those who respond to this new message of the kingdom. Jesus had
told them that with him the kingdom was 'near', 'at hand', 'upon
them'. He was its representative: in him the kingdom of God was

'earthed'. And through him those who repented and believed were brought into that kingdom here and now.

So the disciples of Jesus were to set themselves quite different standards, heavenly ones, and their ambition was not to be confined to earthly goals. The 'nations' may strive for food, clothes, wealth and security—and worry themselves sick about them in the process. His disciples were to 'strive for (God's) kingdom' above all else, and to have done with this corrosive fear. In other words, this new allegiance would be their means of release from daily anxiety.

It's fascinating to see how little the 'menu' of daily worries has changed from the first century to the twenty-first. They were anxious about food, clothing, health, appearance—and so are we, obsessively so in some cases, and with much less reason than they had. Matthew's parallel passage includes an additional popular anxiety—the future: 'So do not worry about tomorrow' (6:34). In my experience, that is probably the greatest single cause of anxiety to modern people—what *might* happen (but probably won't). We worry about loved ones on air flights, about youngsters away at university, about the security of our jobs or about what will happen to us as we grow old.

Jesus asks his disciples to put all of these things into a far grander perspective. You will notice the word 'therefore' in the first verse of this passage. It refers back to his previous warning, at the end of the parable of the rich fool, to those who 'store up treasures for themselves but are not rich towards God'. His disciples are the people of the 'kingdom'—the kingdom of heaven, the kingdom of God. They are not to be dogged by the kind of concerns that blight the lives of those who have not yet shared that vision. There is more to life than money, food, clothes, success, physical beauty, yes, even health itself. And that 'more' is God himself. He is treasure far outweighing these mundane concerns.

As with much of the teaching of Jesus, as we shall see, this is all couched in hyperbolic terms—the use of exaggerated language to heighten the message. This is part of the 'style' of Jesus the teacher—to shock us by stating the case in such extreme terms that we simply can't ignore it. Clearly, he doesn't mean that food, clothing, health and so on don't matter. Indeed, he says very directly that 'your Father knows that you need them' (v. 30). So this is not a call to a life of poverty, hunger and ill health, but a promise that the children of the kingdom, the 'little flock' of their heavenly Father, should trust him to meet their real needs, rather than engage in fruitless and destructive anxiety. After all, as well as the food, clothes and health that they need, 'it is your Father's good pleasure to give you the kingdom'. That, in the end, should be riches enough for anyone.

To REFLECT

The answer to crippling anxiety is not blind optimism ('always look on the bright side of life') but a steadfast trust in the Father's promises. If we are his 'flock' then he is our Shepherd, and the shepherd's task is to ensure that the needs of his sheep are met.

Other passages you may wish to consult: Matthew 6:25–34; Matthew 10:26–31; Luke 12:6, 7

Day 3 (Friday)

Children

MARK 10:13–16

> *People were bringing little children to him in order that he might touch them; and the disciples spoke sternly to them. But when Jesus saw this, he was indignant and said to them, 'Let the little children come to me; do not stop them; for it is to such as these that the kingdom of God belongs. Truly I tell you, whoever does not receive the kingdom of God as a little child will never enter it.' And he took them up in his arms, laid his hands on them, and blessed them.*

Jewish families cherished and valued children, especially—for many practical reasons—boys. But we know from the Gospels that girls were also loved, and perhaps with a degree of affection that exceeded that shown to boys. Jairus, the synagogue official, was clearly distraught at his little daughter's desperate illness, and the sorrow of the family at her apparent death was real and intense (Mark 5:22–43). But male children were vital to the family future, as the guarantors of financial support.

This passage is probably the most 'human' picture of Jesus and children, and has been the subject of many illustrations in children's Bibles! The disciples were understandably worried that Jesus was in danger of being overwhelmed by the crowds who gathered wherever he went, and probably considered this approach by parents on behalf of their children as the last straw. But their stern rebuke to the adults was met by indignant words from Jesus. 'Let the children come to me.' Why? Because it is to 'such as these that the kingdom of God belongs'.

To unravel that statement will take us very near to the heart of the teaching of Jesus, not only about children, but about people and God. The essential qualification for acceptance with God is *dependence*. Faith, trust, obedience, even love for God, flow from our sense that all that we have and all that we are depends on him and him alone. Of that kind of absolute, trusting faith the child is the supreme example.

When the disciples argued among themselves as to which of them was the 'greatest' (a very masculine dispute, it must be said!) Jesus sat them down and used a child as a visual aid. He took the little one in his arms and said to them, 'Whoever welcomes one such child in my name welcomes me, and whoever welcomes me welcomes not me but the one who sent me' (Mark 9:35–37). It was not the *strength* of the disciples that made them citizens of God's kingdom, but their *dependence* on him.

This not only applies to trust. It is also true of wisdom and understanding. The child who accepts the truth without question is always going to have a better access than the rest of us to the deep things of God, which are beyond ordinary human intelligence. 'I thank you, Father,' said Jesus, 'because you have hidden these things from the wise and the intelligent and have revealed them to infants' (Matthew 11:25). This does not mean that we should not use our God-given reason in the search for God's truth, but simply that child-like trust is the key that unlocks the deepest secrets of God when we finally find them. Indeed, it's a recurrent theme of the Bible that unaided human reason simply cannot discover God. 'Can you find out the deep things of God?' Zophar asked Job, clearly expecting the answer 'no'. Truth, in that ultimate sense, is literally 'beyond' us, but the mind of the child—simple, trusting, open—is the model for all of us who pursue it.

However, for Jesus children are more than just visual aids! They are *people*, and people of infinite worth to God. That is why, for him, sin against children is an offence to God. Indeed, 'If any of you put a stumbling block before one of these little ones who believe in me, it would be better for you if a great millstone were fastened about your neck and you were drowned in the depth of the sea' (Matthew 18:6). Harsh words from 'gentle' Jesus!

But it is not only a matter of not abusing children. We are not to despise them either, because 'in heaven their angels continually see the face of my Father' (Matthew 18:10). This idea of 'guardian angels' watching over little children is not just a fanciful illusion, but a demonstration of God's care for the most innocent, dependent and helpless of the human race. We don't necessarily have to think of winged guards at the foot of every bed to see here a proof of the value of the child in the sight of God. We shall fail ourselves, as well as our children, if we do not value them as God does. They are constant reminders of how vulnerable human life is, and of how much we need to trust a heavenly Father.

To REFLECT

How do we value our children, in the family, and, for that matter, in the church? Do we see them as valuable not just in potential, but as sources of wisdom, faith and trust? And do we, like Jesus, welcome them as special people in the kingdom of God?

Other passages you may wish to consult: Matthew 10:37; Matthew 11:25, 26; Matthew 18:6, 7, 10; Mark 9:35–37

DISPUTES & CONFLICT

LUKE 11:17-23

'Every kingdom divided against itself becomes a desert, and house falls on house. If Satan also is divided against himself, how will his kingdom stand?—for you say that I cast out the demons by Beelzebul. Now if I cast out the demons by Beelzebul, by whom do your exorcists cast them out? Therefore they will be your judges. But if it is by the finger of God that I cast out the demons, then the kingdom of God has come to you. When a strong man, fully armed, guards his castle, his property is safe. But when one stronger than he attacks him and overpowers him, he takes away his armour in which he trusted and divides his plunder. Whoever is not with me is against me, and whoever does not gather with me scatters.'

LUKE 9:49, 50

John answered, 'Master, we saw someone casting out demons in your name, and we tried to stop him, because he does not follow with us.' But Jesus said to him, 'Do not stop him; for whoever is not against you is for you.'

The teaching of Jesus on disputes and their resolution is full of difficulties to the modern reader, brought up on the idea of Christ as a healer and reconciler above everything else. It is, of course, absolutely true that he called his followers to 'love your enemies' (Matthew 5:44) and commended the 'peacemakers' as children of God (Matthew 5:9). He also warned that 'all who take the sword will perish by the sword' (Matthew 26:52). Yet the prevailing note of his teaching is one in which the truth *divides*, in which people must make painful choices—choices which will possibly lose them not only friends but even their family. 'I have not come,' he said, 'to bring peace, but a sword. For I have come to set a man against his father, and a daughter against her mother, and a daughter-in-law against her mother-in-law; and one's foes will be members of one's own household' (Matthew 10:34–36). Following him was a matter of 'taking up the cross' and only those willing to 'lose their life' for his sake would 'find it' (see Matthew 10:38, 39).

These are tough words! They probably reflect as much the experience of the early Church as the remembered teaching of Jesus. The first Christians, grappling with opposition and persecution from secular and religious authorities, drew great encouragement from the sayings of Jesus about the conflict and cost of discipleship. But there is also, of course, a timeless truth here, and only those who would want to turn Christianity into some kind of sentimental never-never land will question its authenticity. Truly to follow Jesus is a costly and demanding business, which will cause us pain as well as joy.

The two passages at the head of this chapter set out the apparently contradictory benchmarks very starkly. Both arise from incidents in the ministry of Jesus.

The first followed an exorcism which Jesus performed on behalf of a man who was 'mute'. When the man was healed, two different negative reactions were voiced. Some suggested that Jesus was able to cast out demons because he was in league with the prince of demons, Beelzebul. Others expected him to perform some special 'sign' for their benefit to authenticate his divine authority.

To the first group, Jesus directed a withering argument. What sense was there in the notion that Satan would go around casting out Satan? Strength comes not from division but unity. Divided kingdoms become deserts and divided households collapse (v. 17). That was why (turning the argument around for the second group) Jesus himself demanded unswerving loyalty from his followers: 'Whoever is not with me is against me' (v. 23). Once again we see that oratorical device of driving the argument to its extremes. You must choose where you stand, Jesus says in effect, and if you are not standing with me then you are on the other side. To ask for 'further proof' is simply evidence of a divided loyalty.

The second incident is in sharp contrast. The disciples had seen someone 'casting out demons' in the name of Jesus. They tried to stop him 'because he does not follow with us', and expected Jesus to applaud their action. After all, wasn't he the one who talked about total commitment?

They had, as so often, got it completely wrong. Jesus wasn't interested in building a tight-knit organization with a clearly defined membership consisting only of those who are 'one of us'. He was looking for those who would stand with him in his task, who would hear his word and follow his example. This unidentified person was casting out demons 'in his name', in the name of Jesus of Nazareth. He or she may have got some of the theology wrong—who knows? But their heart was in the right place. They were already on the right 'side' in the conflict. 'Whoever is not against you is for you.'

Just to set out some of these elements of the teaching of Jesus about disputes is to see how complicated an apparently simple exercise can be—and how dangerous simplistic 'summaries' are. Nevertheless, let me now attempt just that!

There are two kinds of dispute. In the first kind, we are asserting our individual 'rights' over against someone else's or trying to exercise power or achieve status at another's expense. In this kind of dispute, 'the least among you shall be the greatest' (see, for example, Luke 9:46–48). Instead of asserting our rights, we take the lower place. Instead of 'lording it' over others, in the manner of the pagans, we are happy to see others succeed. To defend our own rights with violence is self-destructive, as Jesus demonstrated on the occasion of his own arrest in the garden of Gethsemane (see Matthew 26:52).

The second kind of dispute is one in which the truth of God and the values of the kingdom are at stake. Here there can be no room for compromise. 'Whoever is not with me is against me.' Our own pride, or even the correctness of our position, is not the important factor, but the honour of God and his righteousness. On such issues the followers of Christ must be prepared to stand up and be counted, whatever the cost in human terms. Not only is conflict inevitable when people oppose the standards and values of the kingdom, it is a duty for the children of the kingdom. We can 'love' those from whom we have to differ, but we cannot concede the victory to what is essentially evil.

In other words, the *issue* in disputes and conflicts is always the determining factor, not personalities, preferences or pride.

To REFLECT

*When an individual or a church finds itself involved in disputes
and conflict, the question is not 'who is right?' so much as 'what is
at stake?' Is it my pride? The 'correctness' of my position?
My dislike of those who are 'not one of us'? Or is it really the truth
of God and the values of his kingdom?*

Other passages you may wish to consult: Matthew 5:21–26;
Matthew 5:38–45; Matthew 18:15–18; Matthew 26:52; Mark
9:33–35

FIRST WEEK

in LENT

PAUSE *for* PRAYER

MATTHEW 4:4

*Jesus answered, 'It is written, "One does not live by bread alone,
but by every word that comes from the mouth of God."'*

Already, as we have opened ourselves to the teaching of Jesus, we will
have become aware of two emphases that are absolutely typical of his
single-minded approach to truth. One is the authority of God, his
Father: 'It is written...'. He believed that the world was governed by
a purpose. Things, however apparently chaotic, are not out of control.
God is still on the throne of the universe, and what he has purposed
must in the end be fulfilled.

The other is the priority of the spiritual over the material. We tend
to think that material things are 'real' and spiritual things 'unreal' or
illusory. Jesus firmly reverses the priority. The most 'real' thing in the
world is God, and the most important ingredient for life is the 'word
that comes from the mouth of God'.

It's no bad thing from time to time to be challenged by an idea
that cuts right across our ordinary human thinking. Perhaps today,
as we have just embarked on a journey through the teaching of the
Son of God, it would be good to pause and ask ourselves whether we
have become so set on the world's view of things, so entranced by
its values, that we are at times deaf to that life-giving 'word that
comes from the mouth of God'.

A PRAYER

*Lord, challenge my human assumptions; Turn my worldly values
upside-down; Set me free from the slavery of the material world and
its priorities, And help me to pray, as I have never done before,
'Your kingdom come, your will be done on earth, as it is in heaven'.*

The END of the WORLD

MATTHEW 24:29–36

'Immediately after the suffering of those days the sun will be
darkened, and the moon will not give its light; the stars will fall
from heaven, and the powers of heaven will be shaken. Then the
sign of the Son of Man will appear in heaven, and then all the
tribes of the earth will mourn, and they will see "the Son of Man
coming on the clouds of heaven" with power and great glory. And
he will send out his angels with a loud trumpet call, and they will
gather his elect from the four winds, from one end of heaven to the
other. From the fig tree learn its lesson: as soon as its branch
becomes tender and puts forth its leaves, you know that summer is
near. So also, when you see all these things, you know that he is
near, at the very gates. Truly I tell you, this generation will not pass
away until all these things have taken place. Heaven and earth will
pass away, but my words will not pass away. But about that day
and hour no one knows, neither the angels of heaven, nor the Son,
but only the Father.'

Few subjects are given greater emphasis in the teaching of Jesus than
the whole topic of the 'end of the age' or the 'day of the Lord'. The
fact that these concepts are of relatively little concern to most modern
readers has meant that this teaching has become a happy hunting
ground for fanatics of various kinds, who are only too ready to ignore
the warning in this discourse (v. 36) and predict the likely date when
the world as we know it will come to an end.

But it would be a pity if the teaching of Jesus on the final destiny
of the human race were to be ignored simply because fanatics feed on
it. Not only that, but if Jesus himself felt it to be so important, and
devoted so much attention to it, surely his followers should make
some attempt to understand it and apply it in their own generation?

The writings in the Dead Sea scrolls, among other historical
material now available to us, have thrown a great deal of light on
Judaism in the time of Jesus. One of its great concerns, especially

among the 'revivalist' groups that flourished in the desert and along the Jordan valley, was what they called 'the Day of the Lord'. This was the moment, long foretold by the great prophets of Israel (see, for instance, Amos 5:18), when Yahweh, the sovereign Lord, would intervene decisively in the history of the human race. It would signal the end of the present world order and the beginning of the 'new age'. It would be a visible, dramatic and convulsive moment, when the righteousness and justice of God would be revealed, his people vindicated and evil finally overthrown. After three centuries of pagan occupation and religious oppression—and much corruption in the temple and the religious leadership of the nation—the time seemed long overdue for God to *act*.

The passage set out above is the culmination of a long piece of teaching, found not only in Matthew but also (in slightly different forms) in Mark and Luke. The disciples had asked Jesus, 'What will be the sign of your coming and of the end of the age?' (24:3) This discourse, which actually seems to be a collection of various sayings of Jesus on the general subject of judgment and the future, is given as his reply.

The one thing we can be certain about is that this is not meant to be a 'timetable' of future events. This discourse is couched in 'apocalyptic' language, which takes deep truths and expresses them through vivid images and symbols. You can find longer versions of this style of writing in parts of Daniel and the whole of Revelation. To read them in a crudely literal way is to miss the point entirely. 'Apocalypse'—a Greek word meaning 'disclosure', 'illumination', 'unfolding'—offers us a series of signs, symbols and clues, from which the believer is meant to uncover the truth of God's purpose for the world.

Here, Jesus is clearly *not* dealing with a sequence of events in what we might call 'date order'. Some of what he says (vv. 15–28) seems to refer to the immediate future of the Jewish people, and was horribly fulfilled in the destruction of Jerusalem by the Romans in AD70. Some seems to look ahead much further, to a day when the 'good news of the kingdom' will have been proclaimed 'throughout the world' (v. 14) and Jesus, the 'Son of Man', will come again 'with power and great glory' (v. 30). It is the timing of that event that is hidden from human knowledge, and even apparently from Jesus himself (v. 36).

There are also many other sayings about the future, some very general ('wars and rumours of wars', 'famines and earthquakes in various places') and some much more specific (see, for example, verse 15). All include a call to 'readiness'. The believers should be ready at any time for the intervention of God, alert and expectant, so that God's action does not catch them unawares. This, of course, is the message of the story of the wise and foolish virgins (Luke 12:35–40). God operates to his timetable, not ours!

And this is true not just in relation to the future 'Day of the Lord'. In one sense, every occasion when God 'acts' is a 'day of the Lord' for which we should be prepared. The danger is that we get so immersed in the everyday business of life that we fail to see his hand at work. It is the eye of faith that sees in 'ordinary' events the extraordinary activity of God, that 'learns the lesson from the fig tree' (v. 32).

To REFLECT

Can I think of occasions in the past when, after the event, I have become aware that what had happened was not accident, coincidence or chance, but the hand of God? And can I consider how I could be better prepared to recognize such an event for what it is?

Other passages you may wish to consult: Matthew 25:1–13; Mark 13; Luke 12:35–40

FAITH & TRUST

MARK 11:20–24

> *In the morning as they passed by, they saw the fig tree withered away to its roots. Then Peter remembered and said to him, 'Rabbi, look! The fig tree that you cursed has withered.' Jesus answered them, 'Have faith in God. Truly I tell you, if you say to this mountain, "Be taken up and thrown into the sea," and if you do not doubt in your heart, but believe that what you say will come to pass, it will be done for you. So I tell you, whatever you ask for in prayer, believe that you have received it, and it will be yours.'*

On the face of it, this is a ridiculous claim, easily disproved by experience. People with great faith have prayed and believed that their prayer would be answered, but it has not been—at least, not in any form that they can recognize. Not many mountains have been shifted by the power of prayer! So does this mean that Jesus was talking nonsense? Or that he was peddling the kind of 'faith' that bogus healers and other charlatans have promoted?

Clearly not, so there must be another explanation! The trouble for us, reading this with modern eyes, is that we insist on taking the words at their literal meaning, rather than seeing them in the context of the whole of the teaching of Jesus, and the thought-forms and idioms of his day. As we have already seen, Jesus liked to employ the literary device known as 'hyperbole', where exaggerated language is used to emphasize a point—just as we say things like 'It's child's play' (when it clearly isn't) or 'Everything he touches turns to gold' (when in fact all he's done is launch a successful small business). Jesus used this device with great effect, and I have no doubt that his first hearers had no problem understanding what he meant. In the example above, the disciples were astonished that the barren fig tree which Jesus had said would never bear fruit had withered away. 'That's nothing,' he told them, in effect. 'Have faith in God, and you'll see much bigger things that that!'

In the context of the whole teaching of Jesus, 'faith' is *trust in God*. Each of the synoptic Gospels carries as a touchstone a very simple but profound saying: 'With mortals this is impossible, but with God nothing is impossible' (see, for example, Matthew 17:20, Mark 10:27 and Luke 18:27). Faith is not a spell or magic formula to achieve what we want, but a way in to experiencing to the full the power of God—and that is always directed to the fulfilling of his good and perfect purposes. Time and again the Gospels remind us that the only true blessing is 'in the name' of Jesus, according to his will. And the fourth Gospel makes this explicit in regard to prayer: 'I will do whatever you ask *in my name*' (John 14:13).

In other words, those who put their trust in God, who seek to live according to his will, are connected to the ultimate source of power, which is God himself. But it is always and only power to fulfil his will.

'Faith' is a very common word in the teaching of Jesus. Frequently it is connected with healing, where often, though not always, faith was the key to blessing. Sometimes, as we have seen, it is connected to prayer. Sometimes, as when the disciples lost their nerve in a storm on the lake, it is seen as the answer to fear and anxiety. Frequently, Jesus upbraided his disciples for their lack of faith—'you of little faith!' Faith, in this basic sense, is trust in God.

In one magnificent passage of the Sermon on the Mount, Jesus contrasts the pathetic concerns of the world—clothes, food, health, money—with the confidence that flows from faith in God (Matthew 6:19–33). Those who put their trust in money, position and power are building their lives on sand, while those who put their trust in God stand on a rock-like foundation (Matthew 7:24–27).

For Jesus, the outstanding example of faith was the Roman centurion who came to him seeking healing for his servant. What impressed the Lord was the officer's understanding that it was not his rank or position that merited the miracle. Indeed, 'I am not worthy to have you come under my roof.' All he sought from Jesus was that he should 'say the word'—a word of simple command, of the kind that the centurion would speak to his soldiers, or would hear from his own superiors. He understood, in other words, the authority of Jesus, in a way that few if any others had done. 'I tell you,' said Jesus, 'not even in Israel have I found such faith' (see Luke 7:1–10). Faith is not complicated. It isn't an intellectual exercise. It's not a matter of screwing ourselves up and making ourselves believe the impossible. It is a straightforward recognition of the ultimate power and authority of God.

'Lord, increase our faith!' asked the disciples. His reply was to say that even a tiny amount of faith in the right Person—as tiny as a grain of mustard, in fact!—would be enough. It's not the quantity of faith that is crucial, but its *object*. A little faith in a great God is much more effective than mountains of faith in a false one!

To REFLECT

We build faith not by looking at our doubts, or at the problems that confront us, but by looking at God himself. We can't force ourselves to believe, but we can learn to trust.

Other passages you may wish to consult: Matthew 5:33–37; Matthew 8:8–10; Matthew 8:26; Matthew 10:19, 20; Mark 11:24; Luke 17:5, 6

Fasting & Abstinence

MATTHEW 6:16–18

'Whenever you fast, do not look dismal, like the hypocrites, for they disfigure their faces so as to show others that they are fasting. Truly I tell you, they have received their reward. But when you fast, put oil on your head and wash your face, so that your fasting may be seen not by others but by your Father who is in secret; and your Father who sees in secret will reward you.'

LUKE 5:33–35

Then they said to him, 'John's disciples, like the disciples of the Pharisees, frequently fast and pray, but your disciples eat and drink.' Jesus said to them, 'You cannot make wedding guests fast while the bridegroom is with them, can you? The days will come when the bridegroom will be taken away from them, and then they will fast in those days.'

A Victorian poet, Swinburne, described Jesus as the 'pale Galilean'— 'the world has grown grey at his breath'. Now whether he meant it himself, or was putting those ideas in the mouth of another, it's a widely held view that Christianity (and therefore Jesus) is somehow against enjoyment. Plays and novels often depict Christians as puritanical kill-joys, who not only deny themselves the pleasures of life, but go around denying them to everyone else as well.

As we can see from these sayings of Jesus, that wasn't how Jesus saw himself, nor was it how his contemporaries saw him. For them, the real 'puritan' was John the Baptist, with his diet of locusts and wild honey and basic garb of camel skin. By contrast, they found Jesus quite indulgent: a 'glutton and a drunkard' (Luke 7:34). Of course, there is no hint in the Gospels that Jesus was ever drunk, or that he ate food in a gluttonous way, but there's plenty of evidence that he enjoyed a meal with friends and a cup or two of wine.

This is relevant to his teaching on fasting, because here, as in very much of the teaching of Jesus, the emphasis is not on how things seem, but how they are. He wanted to stress that the important thing is inward attitude, not outward show.

Fasting was widely practised by religious people in the time of Jesus. It was seen as a way of self-discipline and self-denial (which was good), and as a way to gain kudos in the community (which was bad). The Pharisees had a complicated system of fasting, which had probably begun as an excellent means of self-discipline but had become, for some of them at least, a matter of public show, with ashes smeared across faces, hair unkempt, and much ostentatious wailing and praying. Jesus roundly condemned this. It was an abuse of the whole principle of fasting as an act of spiritual self-discipline.

For him, a true 'fast' was a matter of inner discipline, which might or might not involve the denial of food or drink, but did involve a private and personal decision about one's relationship with God. This 'secret' decision would be known to God, but no one else, and the 'only' reward would be his blessing.

While Jesus was with them, he did not require his disciples to fast. Indeed, his time with them was one of celebration, rather like the extended party that followed a Jewish wedding! But he recognized that after he had left them, there would be times when fasting would be appropriate (a fact confirmed in the teaching of the early Church—see Acts 13:2 and 1 Corinthians 7:5). But the principle he laid down still holds good for the Christian today. True fasting is fasting of the heart, a private, unforced, voluntary, inner decision to apply a particular discipline in our lives, so that we may be closer to God. It might involve food, or drink, or clothes, or an innocent but time-consuming hobby or interest. Whatever it is, it should never be imposed on us by the rules of others, and it should never show itself in public displays of piety. The modern equivalent to 'put oil on your head' would be a dab or two of make-up (for the women) and a touch of aftershave for the men. Fasting—that is, denying ourselves something that is not in itself wrong, but whose absence will help to concentrate our minds and free our spirits—is meant to be a blessing, not a punishment! Our faith is not given to make us miserable, but to help us to live fulfilled and truly happy lives.

In what ways could modern Christians apply discipline and self-denial to their lives, while following the teaching of Jesus about fasting? How can we build inner discipline, without making a public show of it?

Other passages you may wish to consult: Matthew 9:14–17; Luke 7:33–35

Day 8 (Thursday)

Forgiveness

MATTHEW 18:21–35

*Then Peter came and said to him, 'Lord, if another member of the
church sins against me, how often should I forgive? As many as
seven times?' Jesus said to him, 'Not seven times, but, I tell you,
seventy-seven times. For this reason the kingdom of heaven may be
compared to a king who wished to settle accounts with his slaves.
When he began the reckoning, one who owed him ten thousand
talents was brought to him; and, as he could not pay, his lord
ordered him to be sold, together with his wife and children and all
his possessions, and payment to be made. So the slave fell on his
knees before him, saying, "Have patience with me, and I will pay
you everything." And out of pity for him, the lord of that slave
released him and forgave him the debt. But that same slave, as he
went out, came upon one of his fellow slaves who owed him a
hundred denarii; and seizing him by the throat, he said, "Pay what
you owe." Then his fellow slave fell down and pleaded with him,
"Have patience with me, and I will pay you." But he refused; then
he went and threw him into prison until he would pay the debt.
When his fellow slaves saw what had happened, they were greatly
distressed, and they went and reported to their lord all that had
taken place. Then his lord summoned him and said to him, "You
wicked slave! I forgave you all that debt because you pleaded with
me. Should you not have had mercy on your fellow slave, as I had
mercy on you?" And in anger his lord handed him over to be
tortured until he would pay his entire debt. So my heavenly Father
will also do to every one of you, if you do not forgive your brother
or sister from your heart.'*

It's a long story to serve as the answer to a short question! But it's
such a complete picture of the teaching of Jesus on forgiveness that it
seemed impossible to abbreviate it. Peter spoke of human forgiveness:
how often should he forgive a fellow believer (literally 'brother', in
Greek) who has offended him? Jesus gave him two answers. The first,

very brief, was 'Seventy-seven times'—that is, to infinity (seven being the 'perfect' number). The second answer was, in true Jewish style, to tell him a story.

The story is about a 'lord', but not 'the Lord'. That's quite important! The heart of its message is that one should forgive *because one has been forgiven*. We learn the principle of forgiveness from the experience of being forgiven. And the start of all forgiveness is God's forgiveness of us, which, like the lord's forgiveness of his servant's debt, was undeserved—a pure act of mercy. His 'debt' was cancelled solely through the lord's generosity, activated, perhaps, by what seemed to be true penitence on the part of the servant for his past behaviour.

Yet that same servant then turned on another servant, who owed him a trifling sum. In fact, the figures in the story are fascinating. The first servant owed the equivalent of fifteen years' wages of a labourer —let's say, in modern terms, £120,000. Some debt! The other servant owed a mere day's wage, perhaps £30 or so. There was simply no comparison between the extent of their indebtedness. The crowds listening to this story must have been astonished at the generosity of the lord, and the ingratitude and greed of the forgiven servant. That set them up nicely for the final punchline, of course: 'So my heavenly Father (the *real* Lord) will also do to every one of you, if you do not forgive your brother or sister from your heart.'

Forgiveness was not a major element of Jewish teaching. In fact, the word only occurs once in the whole of the Hebrew scriptures (though the verb 'forgive' is very common). What the Old Testament speaks of most frequently—over a hundred times, in fact—is atonement. Sin can't just be 'forgiven', it must be paid for. The New Testament reverses the emphasis. The word 'forgiveness' occurs many times, but the word atonement only three times, twice referring to Jesus as the one through whom we have 'atonement' for our sins. There is still 'atonement', the 'price of sin' still has to be paid for forgiveness to take place, but Christ has paid it. Forgiveness by God is an act of his perfect generosity, just like the lord in this story. It is not deserved or earned, because it has been paid for by another.

Yet it does incur a debt—a debt of gratitude, that requires us to forgive the sins of others. This is expressed very powerfully in the 'Lord's Prayer'. In Matthew's version we pray, 'Forgive us our debts, as we also have forgiven our debtors.' In Luke it is equally stark: 'And forgive us our sins, for we ourselves forgive everyone indebted to us.' This is echoed in the warning at the end of the story of the unjust servant, which echoes a similar warning at the end of the Lord's Prayer (Matthew 6:14, 15). The key to our forgiveness is our willingness to forgive. Or, to put it another way, if we are not people who forgive, we have not begun to understand the divine principle of forgiveness.

Jesus said that he had 'authority on earth to forgive sins' (Mark 2:10), an authority given to him by his Father. That forgiveness is 'sealed' for us in his blood, which was shed 'for the forgiveness of sins' (Matthew 26:28), a forgiveness we celebrate week by week at the Lord's table. Indeed, according to the teaching of Jesus, 'people will be forgiven for their sins and whatever blasphemies they utter', with the sole exception of the ultimate blasphemy of attributing to Satan the work of God (see Mark 3:28–30). The 'enormous debt' has been paid, and those privileged to be forgiven no longer owe anything except to show their gratitude by extending forgiveness to others. It seems a small price to pay, but it's remarkable how hard we often find it to do.

To REFLECT

To make this teaching personal, I need to spend time considering whether I harbour resentment against anyone else. It is costly to forgive—it cost the Son of God his life—but every time we say the Lord's Prayer we commit ourselves to doing it.

Other passages you may wish to consult: Matthew 6:14, 15; Mark 2:3–12; Luke 7:47–49

DAY 9 (FRIDAY)

GOOD DEEDS

MATTHEW 7:15–21

'Beware of false prophets, who come to you in sheep's clothing but inwardly are ravenous wolves. You will know them by their fruits. Are grapes gathered from thorns, or figs from thistles? In the same way, every good tree bears good fruit, but the bad tree bears bad fruit. A good tree cannot bear bad fruit, nor can a bad tree bear good fruit. Every tree that does not bear good fruit is cut down and thrown into the fire. Thus you will know them by their fruits. Not everyone who says to me, "Lord, Lord," will enter the kingdom of heaven, but only one who does the will of my Father in heaven.'

One of the great themes of the teaching of Jesus, and perhaps especially of Matthew's Gospel, is the danger of a purely nominal discipleship. Here, in this passage, the focus is on 'false prophets'. The test of their authenticity is the moral quality of their lives, just as the quality of a tree—presumably a vine or a fig tree—is the quality of its fruit. No matter how convincing a prophet or attractive his teaching, if his behaviour does not match the standards of the kingdom he is to be rejected.

And what is true of 'prophets' is also generally true. You can find exactly the same words addressed to the Pharisees in Matthew 12:33. In any case, even here it is broadened to include anyone who claims to be a follower of Christ: *anyone* who calls him 'Lord, Lord'. Again, it is 'doing the will of the heavenly Father', not verbal professions of faith, that wins entry to the kingdom of heaven.

Even before Jesus came on the scene, his precursor John the Baptist was hammering home the same message. He warned people coming for his baptism that they should 'bear fruit worthy of repentance'. It was no use their claiming descent from Abraham. That would do them no good at all without the evidence of a life producing (that phrase again!) 'good fruit' (see Matthew 3:7–10).

Good deeds, living the 'righteous' life, are the evidence of true discipleship. That is right at the heart of the message of Jesus. Of course he welcomed 'sinners'. He spoke often, as we have seen, of forgiveness for those who have failed. He was gentle on those who knew they had fallen, but relentless in his challenge of those who thought they were beyond reproach. He was looking not for fine words—then, as now, there were plenty of those—but for pure and kindly actions. Again and again in the Gospels we find him returning to this theme.

For some Christians this poses something of a problem. Surely Christianity is a religion of redemption and forgiveness? Surely we believe that we are saved by the grace of God, rather than our own 'good deeds'? Very knowledgeable people will be aware that the Reformation in the sixteenth century was largely fought over the issue of good deeds ('works', as they were called) versus faith.

Yet really there is no contradiction. Jesus called people to repent (that is, turn from evil) and believe in him. When they did, they would know the forgiveness of God and the gift of eternal life: they would become children of the kingdom of heaven, in the language of the synoptic Gospels. But the evidence that that had happened was not in their profession but in their practice. Tradition has it that James was a brother of Jesus, and certainly his letter echoes many of the teachings of the Sermon on the Mount, from which the passage above is taken. He put the issue very bluntly: 'Faith by itself, if it has no works, is dead... Just as the body without the spirit is dead, so faith without works is also dead' (James 2:17, 26). 'Dead' faith is a profession without practice, claims without commitment, words without witness.

The person whose life is founded on rock is the one who 'hears these words of mine and acts on them,' said Jesus (Matthew 7:24). Faith is required to believe the good news, faith is required to seek God's help rather than trusting in our own resources. But the only valid evidence of that faith is the *difference it makes*.

Good deeds are even more important than keeping the letter of the Law. When a devout rich man came to Jesus and asked him 'what good deed' he must do to have eternal life, he was offered two answers. The first was, 'Keep the commandments.' The man claimed that he had done that 'from his youth'. Then Jesus turned the emphasis on to positive action—not simply avoiding breaking the Law, but going beyond it to 'do good'. 'Go,' he said, 'sell your poss-essions, and give the money to the poor, and you will have treasure in heaven; then come, follow me' (Matthew 19:16–22). The test for this would-be disciple was the test of putting faith into action—and action in the area that was clearly nearest to his heart! He failed the test, and 'went away grieving'.

Good deeds are the evidence of faith as surely as the stars are evidence of the night. Faith makes a difference, and they are the proof of it.

To REFLECT

Through the grace of God I have the gift of eternal life. What kind of life, then, should I lead to demonstrate the work of God in me?

Other passages you may wish to consult: Mark 3:33–35; Luke 6:43–46; Luke 8:15

HEALTH

LUKE 8:43–48

> Now there was a woman who had been suffering from
> haemorrhages for twelve years; and though she had spent all she
> had on physicians, no one could cure her. She came up behind
> him and touched the fringe of his clothes, and immediately her
> haemorrhage stopped. Then Jesus asked, 'Who touched me?' When
> all denied it, Peter said, 'Master, the crowds surround you and
> press in on you.' But Jesus said, 'Someone touched me; for I
> noticed that power had gone out from me.' When the woman saw
> that she could not remain hidden, she came trembling; and falling
> down before him, she declared in the presence of all the people why
> she had touched him, and how she had been immediately healed.
> He said to her, 'Daughter, your faith has made you well;
> go in peace.'

This story, and the healing of the young daughter of Jairus which is
'wrapped around' it, is by far the longest account of a healing miracle
in the Gospels (Matthew, unusually, has a much shorter version). I
have included it in the teaching of Jesus on 'health' because he used
the occasion to say important things about healing, wholeness and
health which have a wider application than to these two specific
cases.

The woman's condition—'menorrhagia', persistent menstrual
bleeding—was not only a serious medical condition, but it effectively
cut her off from human society and religious worship (see Leviticus
15:25–30). So she can serve as an example of the impact of ill health
on people's lives: it causes distress and pain, obviously, but can also
be an isolating and frightening experience. Matthew and Mark—but
not, significantly, the physician Luke—record that she had spent large
sums on ineffective treatment by doctors. That confirms that anxiety
about health is not simply a modern phenomenon!

The story concludes with the woman's simple act of faith in
touching the 'fringe' of his clothes—the 'tassels' of the shawl worn

by devout Jewish men. As she did so, she was healed: she actually felt the haemorrhage stop. Jesus knew that she had touched him because 'power' had left him. This healing, whatever its nature, had cost him something. We can notice that on other occasions extended periods of healing seem to have left Jesus spiritually drained (see, for instance, Mark 1:35).

The healing complete, and the woman having been identified and brought to public notice, Jesus reassured her that all was well: 'Daughter, your faith has made you well; go in peace'. This is almost a formula saying with Jesus—'your faith has healed you' (see, for example, Mark 10:52, in quite different circumstances). Normally (but not always—see Mark 2:1–12) faith was the key to healing in the ministry of Jesus. Indeed, if people didn't or couldn't believe he seems to have been inhibited in his healing work (see Matthew 13:58).

This is not the same thing as what is known as 'faith healing'. People were healed by the power of God working through Jesus; of that there can be no doubt. But usually that healing had to be sought, and it was in that seeking that the sick person showed faith. The healing itself, however, was the work of God, not of the person's 'faith'. Where it was the healing of a specific illness or condition, it was also a gift of God, something that couldn't be deserved or earned (not even by an act of faith), but only received. That is the answer to the 'problem' of unanswered prayer for healing: such healing is God's gift, something we can ask for but not demand. Only God knows what is ultimately for our good and the good of those we love. Faith is content to leave the issue in his hands, in line with his loving purpose.

What Jesus offered to people was healing in the 'holistic' sense—healing of body, mind and spirit. Notice that in this story he said to the woman who had been made well, 'Go in peace.' Being well, healthy, is more than having symptoms treated or an illness 'cured'. It is to be restored to wholeness—the root of the usual word in the New Testament for 'salvation' or 'health'. What Jesus offers is not an insurance policy against illness or disease, but a total life—body, mind and spirit—restored to 'wholeness': becoming more completely what God intends us to be.

Ill health can be caused by many things, including factors outside our control, like our genetic make-up or our childhood nurture. This woman's haemorrhage was almost certainly no fault of her own. But Jesus also linked sickness *in some cases* to sin. The most clear-cut case is the healing of the paralysed man (Matthew 9:2–8). His friends brought him to Jesus, lowering him on a stretcher through the roof. When Jesus saw him lying there paralysed, he said, 'Take heart, son; your sins are forgiven.' This caused something of a furore, partly because Jesus had taken it upon himself to forgive sins (a divine responsibility) and partly because the friends had brought him for healing, not absolution! Jesus proceeded to heal him as well, almost as an afterthought. It seems clear that in this case there was a connection between his paralysis and sin. When he was released from the sin, the paralysis could be cured.

Without in any way endorsing the notion that all ill health is the consequence of individual sin (an idea explicitly rejected by Jesus in John 9:3), it can safely be said that guilt is a negative and corrosive element in human life and the enemy of true health.

The synoptic Gospels show us Jesus the healer at work. Sickness, disease and handicap were regarded as destroyers of human happiness and wholeness, to be confronted by the life-giving Son of God (see Mark 1:41). They are part of life as it is, but not as God intended it to be. But always there is a greater healing lurking, as it were, in the background, and it is in John's Gospel that its nature is expressed in words. Jesus, in dispute with the Jewish teachers, claims that what he offered to people was healing for the whole person (see John 7:23). We are body, mind and spirit, a trinity of elements. To be truly 'well' is for that trinity to be made whole, and *that* is the work of Christ.

To REFLECT

Christ came into the world to bring us 'salvation', that is, to make us completely whole. In what ways do I lack 'wholeness'? What would 'healing for the whole person' mean for me?

Other passages you may wish to consult: Mark 1:40, 41; Luke 4:18,19; Luke 9:11

SECOND WEEK

in LENT

PAUSE *for* PRAYER

JOHN 3:12

Jesus said, 'If I have told you about earthly things and you do not believe, how can you believe if I tell you about heavenly things?'

This is part of the dialogue between Jesus and the Jewish teacher, Nicodemus, who came to see him secretly, by night. Jesus has just used the picture of the wind which 'blows where it chooses, and you hear the sound of it, but you do not know where it comes from or where it goes' as an illustration of the new birth through the Spirit. Nicodemus professes himself baffled: 'How can these things be?' Jesus explains that there is an ascending order of understanding: 'earthly things' leading on to 'heavenly things'. And only through the one who 'descended from heaven, the Son of Man' (v. 13) could that connection be made.

There's a bit of Nicodemus in us all! That's to say, it *is* hard to believe, but we also make it hard for ourselves—'How can these things be?' Instead of trusting the only one who can possibly know—the one who comes to us from God—we struggle to work it all out for ourselves, and all too often fail.

Of course it's right that we should use our God-given intellects to wrestle with the problems of faith, so long as we remember that they are problems of *faith*, which in the end can only be resolved by *faith*. Faith and trust, as we have seen during this past week, are the most vital ingredients of the life of the disciple.

A PRAYER

Lord, increase our faith.
Teach us to trust,
And help us to understand.

HONESTY

MARK 4:21–25

He said to them, 'Is a lamp brought in to be put under the bushel basket, or under the bed, and not on the lampstand? For there is nothing hidden, except to be disclosed; nor is anything secret, except to come to light. Let anyone with ears to hear listen!' And he said to them, 'Pay attention to what you hear; the measure you give will be the measure you get, and still more will be given you. For to those who have, more will be given; and from those who have nothing, even what they have will be taken away.'

I suppose it's hardly surprising that Jesus was in favour of honesty! As we see under many of the headings in this book, a persistent theme of his teaching was the need to do what is 'right', whether in respect of money, debt, our neighbour, those weaker than ourselves or those in authority. Here I want to consider one specific area of honesty, and that is in our commitment to what is *true*.

We might couple with the reading above some words from the Sermon on the Mount: 'Let your word be "Yes, Yes" or "No, No".' Anything beyond that, including the use of extravagant 'oaths', has its origin in evil (see Matthew 5:37). Here we see a principle that underlay not only the teaching but the practice of Jesus where speech was concerned. If he was asked a question, he gave a direct answer— which might be, sometimes, another question, in the Jewish manner! To emphasize a point, he did not call God or heaven or earth to witness, but simply prefaced it with the words, 'Amen, amen'. These are translated 'Verily, verily' in the old versions, and usually something like 'Truly, truly' in the modern ones. 'Amen' means 'so be it', and its repetition adds weight to the assertion: this is true, this is the truth, note it well.

Speaking the truth, then, is a kingdom principle. It is expected of the disciple that he or she will speak the truth, echoing the commandment, 'You shall not bear false witness against your neighbour', but, as in all the teaching of Jesus, taking it further. Christ's disciples will speak the truth because God is a God of truth, because Jesus is 'the truth' (John 14:6) and because he speaks the truth. Over fifty times, the synoptic Gospels use the phrase, 'I tell you the truth' from the lips of Jesus, and exactly the same formula is found twenty-six times in John's Gospel, again employing that little word 'amen'.

Christ's disciples will also speak the truth because to do otherwise is to make oneself liable to exposure. In the end, everything will be revealed: there will be no secrets. In God's sight, nothing is hidden now, but even that which is hidden to human sight will one day be disclosed. Everything will in the end 'come to light'. We can see how true this is in ordinary human experience, when sometimes after many years a scandal is exposed, or an untruth revealed to the public gaze. It is, says Jesus, more than just a 'fact of life'—it is the way God has ordered things. Before him everything will be disclosed, not simply to shame us, but so that deeds done in the dark can be brought into the light and dealt with.

This is in many ways contrary to the spirit of our age, which believes that the truth can be massaged and managed in order to present it in a more 'attractive' light. In ordinary life we speak of 'white lies', untruths designed to flatter or mislead, ostensibly to save someone from hurt. So far as Jesus is concerned, there is simply no substitute for the truth itself. It is self-authenticating. 'There is nothing hidden, except to be disclosed, nor is anything secret, except to come to light.' The principle behind this is set out in the following verses (24, 25), where the openness of truth is the context of what is otherwise a very obscure saying. Those who are open and honest will be treated openly and honestly, and will enjoy a good reputation. Those who try to cover up will lose even the reputation that they have.

In simple language, it's a sort of combination of 'be sure your sin will find you out' (Numbers 32:23) and the old saying 'honesty is the best policy', but it adds an important extra element: honesty is required by a holy God. Christ's disciples are not honest simply because they're afraid of being found out if they aren't, nor because honesty 'pays off' in the end, but because those who 'hunger and thirst for righteousness' are pursuing a kingdom policy.

To speak the truth is the outward sign of an honest heart, and an honest heart is the gift of an honest God. Over and over again Jesus said, 'I tell you the truth'; 'Truly I tell you'; 'Truly, truly'. It was the hallmark of his speech. Those who follow him are set a demanding goal!

To REFLECT

James, the Lord's brother, said, 'Anyone who makes no mistakes in speaking is perfect, able to keep the whole body in check with a bridle' (James 3:2). That seems to echo the teaching of Jesus. What can we do in an age of manipulation of speech, of brainwashing, of subtle advertising and misleading propaganda, to strive for truth? And how can we 'speak the truth'—the whole truth—in our ordinary lives?

Other passages you may wish to consult: Matthew 5:33–37; Matthew 15:8; Luke 8:15–18 (compare Mark: 'what you hear' and Luke: 'how you listen')

Humility

LUKE 14:7–11

When he noticed how the guests chose the places of honour, he told them a parable. 'When you are invited by someone to a wedding banquet, do not sit down at the place of honour, in case someone more distinguished than you has been invited by your host; and the host who invited both of you may come and say to you, "Give this person your place," and then in disgrace you would start to take the lowest place. But when you are invited, go and sit down at the lowest place, so that when your host comes, he may say to you, "Friend, move up higher"; then you will be honoured in the presence of all who sit at the table with you. For all who exalt themselves will be humbled, and those who humble themselves will be exalted.'

Humility is one of the key words to understanding the teaching of Jesus, but just to say that is to risk a deluge of misunderstanding. The teaching of Jesus needs to be interpreted against the model of his life, because we may assume that, of all people, he lived what he taught. If he did, then humility, as he understood it, was not a cringing, cowardly acceptance of the domination of others, nor was it merely a matter of word or gesture ('No, no, you have the best seat, please!')

No one reading the life of Jesus could possibly think of him as cringeing or cowardly. This was the man who singlehandedly drove the traders out of the temple, after all. Nor could we think of the one who silently accepted abuse, scorn and ridicule from those who tried and crucified him, as offering nothing but an outward show of humility. Somehow—and typically—he contrived to balance perfectly a full understanding of who he was with a genuinely humble acceptance of the path of suffering and scorn, when that was called for. 'You call me Teacher and Lord—and you are right, for that is what I am,' he told his disciples (John 13:13). And what was the occasion of that confident claim? It was the moment when he had finished washing his disciples' feet, and it was followed by a call to them to be ready to do the same to each other. This is not exactly how most people think of 'humility', but then Jesus is a complex picture of the truly humble person.

Humility, in the language of the Gospels, is an attitude of mind. When Jesus told his followers to become 'humble', like the child he had set in their midst, he was not asking them to regress to infancy but to become a different kind of adult. What he called for was a conversion of mind, from the natural human instinct to fight for our rights and privileges—'if you don't stand up for yourself no one else will!'—to seeing ourselves as dependent day by day on the grace of God. We are not, in other words, independent masters of our fate but dependent servants of the king—and yet, truly free. Freedom comes from abandoning all those wretched rights and supposed privileges, and humbly (note the word!) waiting for the Lord to call us to the place that he has chosen for us.

As so often, the story expresses it better than the sermon. Invited to a wedding banquet, we don't head for the top table, assuming that we are ahead of others in the distinguished visitor stakes. To do that is to claim privilege. It is also to risk ridicule, because the host may have other ideas about our status. Rather, we cheerfully take the lowest place, and may then experience the honour of being invited to move to a better seat. Or, of course, to be honest, we may be left where we are!

The point of the story is not where we end up, but where we begin: as citizens of the kingdom of God we make no claims, assert no rights, but trust the Lord of the heavenly banquet to lead us into the 'right' place, the place that is 'right' for us.

So humility, in this sense, is an exercise of faith. It's not about assuming we have no worth. In God's sight all of his children are of infinite value, being made in his image. And it's not about 'giving in' to injustice or exploitation. We are to 'hunger and thirst to see right prevail' (Matthew 5:6, REB). But we do it as the dependent, trusting children of God, not as self-appointed warriors of a cause.

The root of the Gospel word for 'humility' is 'poor', 'mean', 'lowly'. It springs from the lowest social group of the day, those who lived on the borderline of survival. From that several words derived which used this condition of physical deprivation to describe a mental attitude. So from that root sprang the words for humble-minded and humility, as well as the verb 'to humble'—oneself, or another. Jesus was himself born into that humble sector of society: Mary spoke of her 'low estate', her 'lowliness' (Luke 1:48). But it is one thing to live in a condition of poverty, which compels us to accept loss of dignity and low status in society. It is quite another voluntarily to make humility our rule of life, and to cultivate, as he did, a gracious and grateful acceptance of our dependence on a loving and generous Father in heaven.

To REFLECT

In a society that honours the achiever and despises the 'failure', how can we cultivate a proper Christian 'humility' without surrendering power to the power-hungry, or denying our own God-given value?

Other passages you may wish to consult: Matthew 18:1–5; Matthew 23:6–12; Mark 6:4; Mark 10:21; John 13:1–16

HYPOCRISY

MATTHEW 23:23-28

'Woe to you, scribes and Pharisees, hypocrites! For you tithe mint,
dill, and cummin, and have neglected the weightier matters of the
law: justice and mercy and faith. It is these you ought to have
practised without neglecting the others. You blind guides! You
strain out a gnat but swallow a camel! Woe to you, scribes and
Pharisees, hypocrites! For you clean the outside of the cup and
of the plate, but inside they are full of greed and self-indulgence.
You blind Pharisee! First clean the inside of the cup, so that the
outside also may become clean. Woe to you, scribes and Pharisees,
hypocrites! For you are like whitewashed tombs, which on the
outside look beautiful, but inside they are full of the bones of
the dead and of all kinds of filth. So you also on the outside
look righteous to others, but inside you are full of hypocrisy
and lawlessness.'

For Jesus, there can be little doubt which was the 'greatest' sin—hypocrisy. In comparison with his scathing denunciation of hypocrites, he opened arms of welcome and forgiveness for the prostitutes and the swindlers. He was dubbed by his enemies 'the friend of sinners' (Luke 15:2), but no one for a moment could have thought of him as the friend of hypocrites.

The Pharisees came in for especially vigorous denunciation, which has led people to suppose that they were at the opposite end of the religious spectrum from Jesus. In fact, that was not the case. On many subjects, including the vital one of the resurrection of the dead, Jesus was on the same side as the Pharisees. Like them, he clearly believed that the problems of Israel were moral and spiritual, not political. Like them, he believed in a disciplined life of prayer and self-denial. Yet they were the constant and fierce target of his wrath—not, one suspects, for what they professed to believe, but for their failure to put it into practice. Too often the Pharisees of his time were more concerned to put on a show than to put on the righteousness of God.

And that, in a nutshell, is a hypocrite. The Greek word means 'play-actor', and thus, by application, someone who plays a part. It's but a step from there to the usual meaning of the word in the New Testament, a moral or religious counterfeit. Jesus hated (the word is not too strong) those who acted out a religious role while disguising motives that were far from religious. He poured scorn on the Pharisees who conducted their times of prayer at street corners, so that everyone would take notice of their piety (Matthew 6:5, 6). 'They have received their reward,' he said. The public might be impressed, but God wasn't.

In the passage above, Jesus is concerned with more subtle brands of hypocrisy. These verses are in the middle of a much longer passage, all to do with the double standards of these religious fanatics (for that is what the Pharisees were). They went to great lengths to keep the Law, even tithing the weeds in their gardens as an offering to God, and meticulously scrubbing the outside of the cup and plate—a reference to their ritual washing of utensils before using them. But they neglected the truly weighty issues: justice, mercy and faith. In this way they stood the truth on its head, and were consequently, as Jesus saw it, a far greater menace than those who clearly opposed or ignored God's law.

As usual, Jesus the Jew has a story for it, the well-known sketch of the archetypal hypocrite. Although he has a log wedged in his own eye, he is more concerned about the speck of dust in his neighbour's, which he is anxious to remove (Matthew 7:3–5). 'You hypocrite,' comments Jesus, 'first take the log out of your own eye, and then you will see clearly to take the speck out of your neighbour's eye.' Like many profound truths, it is so obvious that we frequently overlook it.

Hypocrisy didn't start and end with the Pharisees. Indeed, it would be safe to say that there's a bit of the Pharisee in most religious people! There can't be many Christians, for instance, who would claim that their inner life has always matched the splendour of their outward profession. One of the most common objections to Christianity is that 'all Christians are hypocrites'. It's one of those 'well-known facts' that makes it all right for people to distance themselves from the Church. And obviously there's a certain element of truth in it. Yet those who are sincerely trying to follow Jesus will be most aware of the danger of hypocrisy, and should be the first to recognize its subtle inroads.

Yet the teaching of Jesus demands that we don't let things drift, simply because we are all liable to failure and are all constantly in need of forgiveness. The sincere intention to match what we 'believe in our hearts' with what we 'show forth in our lives' (to quote the old prayer) is an essential part of discipleship. The Lord who welcomed the openly sinful seemed to find it much harder to accept the openly self-righteous! Yet hypocrisy, too, can be repented, rejected, struggled against—and forgiven. If it were not so, there would be no gospel for most of us!

To REFLECT

In what areas of my own life is there a conflict between the nobility of what I profess to believe and the reality of the way I live?

Other passages you may wish to consult: Matthew 7:3–5; Matthew 12:33–35; Matthew 16:6–12; Matthew 21:12, 13; Luke 11:37–40; Luke 12:1–3

Day 14 (Thursday)

Joy

MATTHEW 5:3−12

'Blessed are the poor in spirit, for theirs is the kingdom of heaven.
Blessed are those who mourn, for they will be comforted. Blessed
are the meek, for they will inherit the earth. Blessed are those who
hunger and thirst for righteousness, for they will be filled. Blessed
are the merciful, for they will receive mercy. Blessed are the pure in
heart, for they will see God. Blessed are the peacemakers, for they
will be called children of God. Blessed are those who are persecuted
for righteousness' sake, for theirs is the kingdom of heaven. Blessed
are you when people revile you and persecute you and utter all
kinds of evil against you falsely on my account. Rejoice and be
glad, for your reward is great in heaven, for in the same way they
persecuted the prophets who were before you.'

The Greek word which is translated 'blessed' here is *makarios*—yes,
the same as the name of that Cypriot archbishop and president whom
older readers will remember for his role in the troubles on that island
forty years ago. Its literal meaning is 'happy', which, by extension,
and especially in Jewish thought, means 'blessed by God'. In Latin
the word here is *beati*, which gives us our English word 'Beatitudes',
the name often given to these famous sentences from the lips of Jesus.

They speak, then, of those qualities or attitudes which lead to true
happiness or 'blessedness', and they end with an exhortation to
'rejoice', to be full of 'joy'. So far, so good. But when one looks at the
passage, it is disconcerting to discover that the qualities which Jesus
sees as paths to happiness would be considered by most of us as paths
to abject misery. How can the bereaved be 'happy'? Or those strug-
gling for justice? Or those who are 'poor in spirit', persecuted, reviled
and falsely accused? By what twist of logic can these conditions be
seen as gateways to joy?

The first answer to that objection is, as so often, to stop looking at
these first-century Jewish sayings as though they are twenty-first-

century Western ones. This kind of 'wise word', based on a daring paradox, was a familiar style of rabbinic wisdom. And paradox is the clue to it—putting together two apparently contradictory ideas, and yet forging from that combination an insight of astonishing wisdom.

For instance, how can those who mourn be described as 'happy'? It was no less true then than now that bereavement is the single most desolating and isolating human experience. Of course Jesus wasn't suggesting that those who mourn were full of the joys of life, 'happy' in the sense of laughing and relaxed. What he was saying, however— and the truth is best revealed by switching round the phrases of the saying—was that those who mourn will be comforted (literally, given strength), and *therefore* they are 'happy', 'blessed'.

We can treat others of these sayings in the same way. Those who are poor in spirit (that is, those who know they are not self-sufficient, who depend only on God) will have the kingdom of heaven: *therefore* they are 'happy', 'blessed'. Those who are merciful will receive (God's) mercy: *therefore* they are happy. Those who are pure in heart will see God: *therefore* they are happy.

The paradox reaches its climax in the final beatitude, which calls on those who are reviled, persecuted and slandered to 'rejoice and be glad'—a ludicrous concept, in ordinary human logic! But Jesus gives the reason: 'Great will be your reward in heaven.' The values of the kingdom are not the values of the world. Indeed, they are its opposites. True happiness, in other words, is not dependent on circumstances but on our relationship with God himself, from whom all true happiness and blessedness flow. This is the 'joy in heaven' which Jesus said results from the repentance of a single sinner, the recovery of one lost 'sheep' (see Luke 15:7, 10, 32).

There is every evidence that Jesus, far from being a sombre, digni-fied kind of person, exuded an attractive joy. His path through Galilee, certainly, seems to have been marked by an infectious happi-ness, which the crowds contrasted with the aesthetic and sober style of John the Baptist (see, for instance, Luke 7:31–35). At the wedding in Cana of Galilee, one suspects that John might have preferred to turn the wine into water!

But the joy of Jesus was not a light, frothy thing, easily dissipated by changed circumstances. It was a deep sense of fulfilment, of being at one with the purpose of the Father (see Hebrews 12:2). This is the joy and happiness that comes from true faith, from knowing that those who mourn will be comforted, the poor in spirit will inherit the kingdom, the meek will inherit the earth.

To REFLECT

To seek joy for itself is an elusive and often disappointing experience. Joy, in the teaching of Jesus, is a by-product of faith, of depending totally and wholly on the grace of God, and seeking to fulfil his purpose for us. How can that truth become real for an age that is desperate for 'happiness' but reluctant to accept that it can ultimately come only from seeking the will of God?

DAY 15 (FRIDAY)

JUSTICE

LUKE 18:2-8

He said, 'In a certain city there was a judge who neither feared God nor had respect for people. In that city there was a widow who kept coming to him and saying, "Grant me justice against my opponent." For a while he refused; but later he said to himself, "Though I have no fear of God and no respect for anyone, yet because this widow keeps bothering me, I will grant her justice, so that she may not wear me out by continually coming."' And the Lord said, 'Listen to what the unjust judge says. And will not God grant justice to his chosen ones who cry to him day and night? Will he delay long in helping them? I tell you, he will quickly grant justice to them. And yet, when the Son of Man comes, will he find faith on earth?'

This is a strange story in some ways—very strange if the reader makes the mistake of thinking that the judge in the story represents God! We don't 'get what we want' in prayer, and certainly not by nagging God. In fact, despite Luke's introduction, which seems to imply that it is a parable about the 'need to pray always and not to lose heart', this parable is essentially about the human cry to God for justice. The widow can stand for all people treated unjustly: the exploited, the oppressed, the abused, those who starve in the midst of plenty and those who rot in prison under corrupt legal systems. The judge stands for those who have the power to right wrongs—literally, here, to 'vindicate' the cause of those who suffer through injustice. The Lord's point is that in the end, through human pressure and the threat of public exposure, he *may* bring about justice. But *how much more* (a favourite expression of Jesus) will a God whose very nature is justice 'grant justice to his chosen ones who cry to him day and night'? The whole point of the story is the vivid comparison of opposites: corrupt human justice, of which the Jewish people of the time had daily experience, and the perfect justice of God.

Yet the problem remains: if God will 'quickly grant justice', why does it seem to us to be so long coming? Why do tyrants prosper and die in their beds, while the oppressed continue to suffer and the victims of injustice are not vindicated? Why does it seem that God 'delays long in helping them'? There seems to be a hint of the answer in verse 8: 'And yet, when the Son of Man comes, will he find faith on earth?'

The choice of the word 'faith' is fascinating! Why not 'justice' or 'righteousness'? Faith is trust in God. The implication seems to be that because God's justice *is* long delayed (on human timetables), faith will wear thin, so that on the Day of the Lord, when Jesus returns to bring in God's kingdom, it may have evaporated to vanishing point! The call of this story, then, is to strengthen faith—faith that God hears the cries of the oppressed and that he has already granted them vindication, though that has not yet been seen or acknowledged by human eyes.

That may seem a bit tortuous, though it probably spoke more powerfully to a people who had been under a foreign yoke for three hundred years and struggled to retain a faith in God's purpose for them. Yet it tells us one vital thing about the nature of God: he is a God of justice, totally committed to justice, not only as a principle but in practice.

Here the 'justice' Jesus spoke of is vindication—the righting of wrongs. Elsewhere he spoke of justice in the sense of what is fair and equitable. The people of the kingdom should not need magistrates—even good ones!—to force them to concede what is right and fair to others. They should live by the very principle of fairness. 'Why do you not judge for yourselves what is right?' Jesus asked his disciples. 'Thus, when you go with your accuser before a magistrate, on the way make an effort to settle the case'—don't wait for the worldly systems of law to compel you to do what you already know to be right (Luke 12:57–59).

Applied to modern life, the consequences are very challenging. Many of us have no qualms about not paying taxes or other dues until we are compelled. And how many of us would voluntarily pay what we 'know to be fair' if we thought the Inland Revenue had overlooked it? In disputes over bills or charges, are we inclined to demand our 'rights' or to try to act according to the justice of God? And what about Third World debts—debts owed, in effect, to *us*, by some of the poorest people on earth? How are we meant to 'judge for ourselves what is right' when the questions of justice posed by the modern world are so complex and confusing?

I think the answer of Jesus would be that the *intention* is all. To do what is just and right is a fundamental requirement by God of his people: 'What does the Lord require of you but to do justice, and to love kindness, and to walk humbly with your God?' (Micah 6:8) The teaching of Jesus on justice is simply the application of that requirement to our present lives, together with a confident trust that if we do that, ultimate justice lies in God's hands, and will be revealed in his own good time.

To REFLECT

What does it require of us to 'do justice' in a fundamentally unjust world? How can Christians struggle for justice on behalf of others, but sit more lightly to demanding justice for themselves? And is it not too simple to counter the accusation that God does nothing about present injustice by inviting people to 'wait and see'?

Other passages you may wish to consult: Matthew 7:1, 2; Luke 12:57–59; Luke 12:13–15

KINGDOM *of* HEAVEN

LUKE 13:18–21

He said therefore, 'What is the kingdom of God like? And to what should I compare it? It is like a mustard seed that someone took and sowed in the garden; it grew and became a tree, and the birds of the air made nests in its branches.' And again he said, 'To what should I compare the kingdom of God? It is like yeast that a woman took and mixed in with three measures of flour until all of it was leavened.'

LUKE 17:20, 21

Once Jesus was asked by the Pharisees when the kingdom of God was coming, and he answered, 'The kingdom of God is not coming with things that can be observed; nor will they say, "Look, here it is!" or "There it is!" For, in fact, the kingdom of God is among you.'

This book is about the teaching of Jesus, and I suppose it could all be summed up in four words: 'the kingdom of God'—though that would make a very thin book! The 'kingdom' is the theme of the message of Jesus. He preached 'the good news of the kingdom' (Matthew 9:35). It was the goal he held up before his disciples: 'Strive first for the kingdom of God' (Matthew 6:33). Time and again he returned to it, in story and sermon. Indeed, in him, he said, the 'kingdom of God had come' (Matthew 12:28).

The 'kingdom of God' and the 'kingdom of heaven' (which is how Matthew often refers to it) are one and the same concept. In the synoptic Gospels there are well over 140 references to the 'kingdom'. In John there are just four—for him, 'eternal life' seems to speak of much the same vision. The early Christians preached the 'good news of the kingdom' (see, for example, Acts 8:12). So if we wish to understand the message of Jesus, we must grapple with this slightly elusive notion of the kingdom of God.

It is more difficult for the modern reader simply because we have little or no experience of what a 'kingdom' in this sense is. Modern kingdoms are mostly constitutional monarchies, where the power of the king or queen is strictly circumscribed by constitution and the democratic process. When Jesus spoke of a 'kingdom', his hearers had in mind the image of the absolute ruler, whose writ ran without question from one end of his territory to the other. The king was both the law maker and the law enforcer. He set the laws, he applied their penalties, and he was the only point of appeal. A kingdom was, in other words, where the king reigned, where his will was done.

There were, of course, good kings (though not, judging by the Hebrew experience, very many!). But it was deep in the Jewish vision of government that the only true king was the Lord, that he was the source and model of kingly rule: 'By me kings reign' (Proverbs 8:15). Earthly kings might be weak, indecisive, corrupt, brutal and unjust, but 'kingship' could still be a picture of the rule of God, because his rule was everything that their rule was *not*. The rule of God is strong, decisive, fair, gentle and just; yet, in the pattern of absolute monarchy, it is also absolute. If we are within the kingdom of God we are under the rule of God. And Jesus came to call people to enter, by repentance and faith, into that kingdom and to put themselves under that rule.

So the kingdom of God is not so much a place as a state of mind—a state of full and voluntary submission to the will of the good king. Jesus could say that the kingdom of God was present in him because he perfectly, fully and voluntarily submitted to the will of his heavenly Father. All who submit are its subjects, and its boundaries are the limits of their company. In other words, you can't draw its borders on a map (as people once tried to do with 'Christendom'), but they are known to God, and include everyone everywhere who submits to his just and gentle rule. A kingdom is the defined area where a monarch reigns, so the kingdom of God is where God reigns. That seems to be the point of the answer Jesus gave to the Pharisees. The kingdom can't be 'observed', because it is 'among' (or, according to the footnote, 'within') you. Being in God's kingdom is a matter of interior obedience, not outward registration!

But being in God's kingdom involves responsibilities. To live under the rule of God is to seek to live our lives according to his require-ments, to fulfil his purpose for our own lives and the whole world.

That's a high and exciting calling: to be part of God's great purpose of love for the whole of his creation. Christians are kingdom people living by kingdom principles, not simply for their own salvation but for the blessing of the whole world.

The two examples of kingdom parables at the start of this chapter —chosen almost at random from dozens of others—emphasize the same point. The mustard seed and the yeast are insignificant in themselves, but nurtured in the right environment (the 'kingdom of heaven') they become powerful, influential and irresistible. As individual Christians, we may not think our influence in the world amounts to a row of beans, yet planted in the soil of the kingdom, and seen as part of God's magnificent purpose for everything, the tiny seed can grow into a tree and the trace of yeast infiltrate the whole batch of loaves. At this very moment the world is a better place because of the presence of the kingdom and its people; only faith can imagine what it will one day be when 'his kingdom has come, and his will is done on earth, as it is in heaven'.

To REFLECT

The idea of the kingdom holds out the wonderful prospect for the Christian of a new kind of life, in a new kind of community, with a new kind of values and a new kind of purpose. Does a highly individual notion of salvation detract from that magnificent vision? How can we fit the call to individual repentance and faith into the great purpose of God for his whole creation? Am I 'saved' for a purpose that is beyond my own salvation?

Other passages you may wish to consult: Matthew 12:28; Mark 1:15; Mark 4:26–29; Luke 10:8–11; Luke 13:29, 30; Luke 14:15–24

THIRD WEEK

in LENT

PAUSE *for* PRAYER

JOHN 4:10

Jesus answered her, 'If you knew the gift of God, and who it is that is saying to you, "Give me a drink", you would have asked him, and he would have given you living water.'

This is part of the conversation of Jesus with the Samaritan woman at Jacob's well. He has asked her to draw him some water from the well and she has expressed surprise that a Jew should make such a request of a Samaritan. The words above are Jesus' response—enigmatic (in the style of John's Gospel), and full of spiritual imagery.

It is the phrase 'living water' that stands out. The water in the well was standing water, possibly even rather stagnant. Jesus suggests that he could give her spring water (living water), water that bubbles effervescently, that is tangy on the palate and refreshingly cool. It is an image that will recur in John's Gospel several times. Jesus is the water of life, water that gives life. Perhaps we need to live in a dry, hot land to capture the full appeal of those words.

We were thinking yesterday about the kingdom of heaven, the place where God's will is perfectly fulfilled in justice, love and peace. In the beautiful image of heaven in the last chapter of Revelation, there flows through its streets 'from the throne of God' a 'river of the water of life, bright as crystal' (22:1). Where God is on the throne, where his will is done, the life-giving water flows. 'In your right hand are pleasures for evermore (Psalm 16:11).' In a real sense, this is the 'meaning' of heaven.

A PRAYER

'Lord, give me this water, so that I may never be thirsty.'

LAW

MATTHEW 5:17–20

'Do not think that I have come to abolish the law or the prophets; I have come not to abolish but to fulfil. For truly I tell you, until heaven and earth pass away, not one letter, not one stroke of a letter, will pass from the law until all is accomplished. Therefore, whoever breaks one of the least of these commandments, and teaches others to do the same, will be called least in the kingdom of heaven; but whoever does them and teaches them will be called great in the kingdom of heaven. For I tell you, unless your righteousness exceeds that of the scribes and Pharisees, you will never enter the kingdom of heaven.'

This passage could be called Jesus' 'policy statement' on the law. It sets out very clearly where he stands in relation to 'the law and the prophets', and in what way his understanding of them would take people further into their true fulfilment. It is pure fiction to suggest that Jesus was 'anti-law', or set out to overthrow all that God had revealed to Israel as his purpose for human happiness and fulfilment. But he wanted his disciples to move beyond observing the 'law' as the 'scribes and Pharisees' did, as a set of ceremonial and disciplinary requirements. For him, the law of God is the ruling principle of the kingdom of heaven. Those who 'do and teach' God's commandments will be 'called great in the kingdom'. Those who break—or, more literally, try to 'annul'—the commandments will be 'least' in the kingdom.

The fact that he had to tell his followers *not* to think that he had come to 'abolish the law or the prophets' suggests that he was being accused of doing precisely that! His less than strict attitude to the observance of the sabbath (see, for instance, Mark 2:23–27), and his trenchant attack on the Pharisees for their nit-picking over tithes (see Luke 11:42), may have given people the impression that he regarded the law of the Hebrew scriptures as no longer relevant. If people had thought that, then these words should have dispelled the idea. 'I have not come to abolish but to *fulfil*' (v. 17). In his teaching, he is claiming, all that the law sought and struggled to do can be brought to completion.

To understand this, we have to understand something of the role of 'the law' in Jewish thought. The single word 'law' actually covers a huge range of concepts: ceremonial law (mostly found in Leviticus) —instructions about worship, sacrifices and so on; criminal law, much of it found in Exodus, relating to offences and their punishment; moral law, which laid down principles of human behaviour ('You shall love the Lord your God with all your heart, mind, soul and strength', Deuteronomy 6:5) and family law, relating to marriage, divorce, widows and so on. The Ten Commandments (Exodus 20) are a summary of the law of God, setting out the principles that lay behind God's relationship with his people of the covenant.

All of this was fine, so far as it went. But over the centuries, like every legal system, it had fallen into the hands of the lawyers! From a relatively straightforward set of principles, the law had become an enormous and complicated compilation of hundreds and hundreds of 'clarifications', additions, explanations and additional clauses, so that ordinary people could not hope to understand it, and had to rely on the teaching of so-called 'experts'—the much-maligned 'scribes' of New Testament times. From a set of divine principles for a holy life and a holy community, they had become a set of rules to be kept— or, if possible, avoided by hundreds of clever get-out clauses. Jesus refers to one such 'get-out' clause in his attack on the Pharisees (see Mark 7:11).

We can see in the passage, and in what follows it in this discourse by Jesus, that he was committed to the *principle* of the law, but wanted to reform its *practice*. And that 'reformation' was consistently in one direction: away from outward observance, and towards inward conversion of heart. This is probably best understood by studying the examples that follow (see Matthew 5:21–43). He takes six of the most fundamental laws of the Hebrew scriptures (what Christians call the 'Old Testament'): against murder and adultery, and concerning divorce, the taking of oaths, retaliation and human relationships. In each case he follows exactly the same procedure, restating the law (with the formula, 'You have heard that it was said to those in ancient times...') and then giving his 'new' application or interpretation of it: 'But I say to you...'). And in each case the effect of his interpretation is to transform a law about outward behaviour into a matter of interior conversion.

So it is not enough simply to avoid murder; the people of the kingdom will seek to eradicate anger from their lives (v. 22). It is not enough simply to abstain from adultery. Christ's followers will seek a life of inner purity of thought (v. 28). It is not enough to restrict revenge to a proportionate response—'an eye (but no more than an eye) for an eye'; his disciples will reject the whole idea of vengeance, and seek to live generously and with forgiveness in their hearts (vv. 38–42). And so on: the new principle can be employed to reinterpret each of the 'old' laws in a way that brings out the true divine purpose behind them.

This is a radical new approach, and it is not surprising that it was this, more than anything else, that brought opposition from the religious authorities to Jesus. He was denounced as a law-breaker, and one who encouraged others to do the same. But in fact he was rescuing that very law from the dead weight of tradition, transforming it from a set of rules for outward observance into a set of principles for training and guiding the human heart into the ways of God. That was what the 'law' had always been at its best (see, for instance, Psalm 119:10–16)—a way of life, a joy, a window into the very mind of God.

To REFLECT

Which would we rather have: a set of rules to keep (or break), or a set of principles that can convert our hearts to the way of God? That is really the choice which Jesus set before his disciples, and sets before us.

Other passages you may wish to consult: Matthew 12:1–6; Matthew 12:11–13; Matthew 22:34–40; Mark 2:23–27; Mark 3:1–6

DAY 18 (TUESDAY)

LOVE

MATTHEW 22:34–40

> *When the Pharisees heard that he had silenced the Sadducees, they gathered together, and one of them, a lawyer, asked him a question to test him. 'Teacher, which commandment in the law is the greatest?' He said to him, ' "You shall love the Lord your God with all your heart, and with all your soul, and with all your mind." This is the greatest and first commandment. And a second is like it: "You shall love your neighbour as yourself." On these two commandments hang all the law and the prophets.'*

Writing about twenty years after Jesus spoke these words, the apostle Paul provided the perfect commentary on them: 'Love is the fulfilling of the law' (Romans 13:10). The religious teachers of our Lord's time, as we have seen, were intent on reducing law to a matter of dos and don'ts: observe this ritual, pay this tithe, offer this sacrifice, say this prayer, give these alms. Jesus lifts the whole debate on the law to a higher plane, as we have seen. For him, if we have learnt the true meaning of love, then we have met every requirement of the law.

The context of this famous saying of Jesus is, as so often, the reply to a question intended to trick him into a theological indiscretion. The Pharisees had watched Jesus see off the Sadducees, who had tried to floor him with a question about the resurrection of the dead, which they did not believe in. Now they thought they were on safer ground. By inviting Jesus to elevate one law above another, they hoped to show that, conversely, he valued some laws less than others. His reply was, as usual, both brilliant and unanswerable, because he went to the very foundation of the whole principle of divine law. If his argument was true, then all law derives from the one principle of love. We keep the law out of love for God, who gave it, and our neighbour, for whose good it was intended.

But in answering a question about law, Jesus also gave us his great interpretation of love. For him, love is never selfish and self-centred. It doesn't, and cannot, say 'I love you and I want you and I'm going to have you.' That is not love but possession! True love mirrors the love of the creator himself, who made us in his image and furnishes us with everything we need for life, love and happiness. We are to love him with 'heart, mind and soul'—with the whole person, in other words. Our love for God is intellectual, as we grasp the wonder of his generosity and mercy. It is emotional, as we respond to his loving care; and it is spiritual, as we relate to his Spirit at work in us. Every part of our being can and should rise up to express our love for God.

And that love then overflows into love for our fellow creatures— and, for once, that is precisely the right description. Because we are all his offspring, all made in his image, all bearing the ineradicable stamp of his nature (however spoiled and tarnished), we recognize in our 'neighbour' the love of God and, for God's sake, extend love to him or her. There can be no picking and choosing here! God's love is indiscriminate. He 'makes his sun rise on the evil and on the good, and sends rain on the righteous and on the unrighteous' (Matthew 5:45). It is to follow the example of our heavenly Father, argues Jesus, that we learn to love our enemies, for hasn't he done exactly that? 'If you love those who love you, what reward do you have?' (5:46). To be 'children of your heavenly Father' involves taking after the Father and loving even our enemies (5:44), for they too are our 'neighbours'.

In the Gospels, disciples are charged to show love in three dimensions: to God, to our neighbour, and to our enemy. We love God because he is worthy of our love. We love our neighbour because we see something of God in him or her, and respond to their human need (see Luke 10:37). And we love our enemy because in that way we share in and express the indiscriminate love of the Father, who does not love us because we are 'lovable' but because he *is* love.

This is a very lofty concept of love, which we may well feel is beyond human achievement. After all, most of us find it quite hard to love our neighbour, let alone our enemy! But it is consistent with the whole direction of the teaching of Jesus that he should set before the people of the kingdom high and lofty goals. 'Be perfect, therefore, as your heavenly Father is perfect' (Matthew 5:48). We are, in a phrase used by a woman in a discussion group at our church the other night, 'pursuing Christians'—pursuing high goals, pressing towards the mark, striving to become what God intends us one day perfectly to be. Now we seek to love as best we can. One day we shall know the perfection of love. But the one is the eventual consequence of the other. Those who seek, find.

To REFLECT

'Kingdom love' is as different from the world's idea of love as we can imagine. Kingdom love gives; the world's love takes. Kingdom love serves; the world's love demands. Kingdom love is not selective; the world's love is exclusive, and expects love in return. Kingdom love is 'the fulfilling of the law', because those who love like this are already living far beyond the letter of the law.

Other passages you may wish to consult: Matthew 5:43–48; Luke 10:25–28; Luke 7:40–47; John 13:34, 35

MARRIAGE, SEX & SELF-CONTROL

MATTHEW 5:27–32

'You have heard that it was said, "You shall not commit adultery."
But I say to you that everyone who looks at a woman with lust has
already committed adultery with her in his heart. If your right eye
causes you to sin, tear it out and throw it away; it is better for you
to lose one of your members than for your whole body to be thrown
into hell. And if your right hand causes you to sin, cut it off and
throw it away; it is better for you to lose one of your members than
for your whole body to go into hell. It was also said, "Whoever
divorces his wife, let him give her a certificate of divorce." But I say
to you that anyone who divorces his wife, except on the ground of
unchastity, causes her to commit adultery; and whoever marries a
divorced woman commits adultery.'

To judge by the obsessions of the Church down the centuries, and even of preachers and religious periodicals today, you would think that the teaching of Jesus on the subject of sex and marriage was extensive. In fact, as even a quick reading of the Gospels will confirm, Jesus had relatively little to say on a subject which is of such consuming interest to the modern world. Apart from this single (but very powerful and challenging) statement about the destructive power of lust, he said nothing about the control of the human sex drive. And on the subject of marriage, we have this, and parallel, references to the permanence of marriage in God's purpose, but nothing else.

Indeed, in action as well as words Jesus seems to have been much more concerned about the 'spiritual' sins of pride, ambition and hypocrisy than about the so-called 'sins of the flesh'. His openness and welcome to 'sinners' included, we are told, the prostitutes, who would go into the kingdom of heaven before the self-righteous priests and elders (see Matthew 21:23, 31, 32). Two stories in John's Gospel, of the woman taken in adultery (8:1–11) and of the immoral

Samaritan woman at Jacob's well (4:7–30), show a remarkable degree of understanding and mercy, without in the slightest degree condoning their behaviour. And the incident at the home of a Pharisee again shows the gentleness of Jesus towards a woman 'who was a sinner'— presumably, a prostitute (see Luke 7:36–50).

It's worth asking ourselves why the Gospels should reveal this emphasis. After all, the Jewish society of our Lord's day was very strict about sexual behaviour—we would say 'puritanical'—and those who departed from conventional morality were treated as outcasts. Yet these are the very people whom Jesus made the focus of his ministry, so that the complaint went up, 'This fellow welcomes sinners and eats with them' (Luke 15:2). It is impossible to argue that Jesus viewed sexual immorality as trivial: the passage at the head of this chapter would be enough to refute that view. Nor did he take the marriage bond lightly. For him, the divine principle 'from the first' was absolutely clear: one man, married to one woman, for life, because they have become in marriage 'one flesh' (Mark 10:8).

In fact, in this as on other matters Jesus set before his disciples conditions that they regarded as beyond human attainment. 'If such is the case of a man with his wife' (that is, that he may not divorce her and marry another), the disciples complained to Jesus, 'it is better not to marry.' His reply to them is revealing: 'Not everyone can accept this teaching, but only those to whom it is given' (Matthew 19:10, 11). In other words, the children of the kingdom would be expected to set themselves higher goals than those who were outside it. Those goals might seem impossible to attain ('you shall be perfect'), but they stood as the standards of God himself, and Jesus was not going to water them down for public approval.

But at the same time—and this, I think, is the 'meaning' of the stories of Jesus with those who have fallen into sexual sin—there is always the offer of forgiveness and a new life to those who repent. *Admission of failure* is the key to this, and the sin of the self-righteous was their utter refusal to see themselves as other than paragons of virtue. That was why the prostitutes would enter the kingdom of heaven ahead of them: the prostitutes knew about guilt, sorrow for sin, repentance and forgiveness. They had no problem over 'admission of failure'. But the Pharisees and their ilk were blind to such things.

For the children of the kingdom, however, the highest standard is set. Nothing less than a pure heart, pure eyes, pure motives—leading inevitably to pure actions. In the passage above, Jesus is not advocating self-mutilation in the interests of sexual purity, as some ascetics have done in the past. He is holding before his disciples the relative value of an eye or a hand when compared to the riches and joy of the kingdom of heaven. Self-control is very often a matter of priority—what really matters to us, what our chief aim and objective is. If we get the goal right, Jesus argues, then eventually, with God's help, we shall get the whole of life right.

To REFLECT

In a society apparently obsessed with sex, and with the idea of sexual freedom, how can we convey the teaching of Jesus about self-control, faithfulness in marriage, and the goal of inner purity? At the same time, how can we share in his welcoming love and acceptance of those who have failed to live a life of purity? Indeed, how can we find acceptance for ourselves in his welcome to the 'sinners'?

Other passages you may wish to consult: Matthew 19:3–13; Luke 7:31–50; John 4:7–30 and 8:1–11

DAY 20 (THURSDAY)

MONEY & POSSESSIONS

MATTHEW 6:19–24

'Do not store up for yourselves treasures on earth, where moth and rust consume and where thieves break in and steal; but store up for yourselves treasures in heaven, where neither moth nor rust consumes and where thieves do not break in and steal. For where your treasure is, there your heart will be also. The eye is the lamp of the body. So, if your eye is healthy, your whole body will be full of light; but if your eye is unhealthy, your whole body will be full of darkness. If then the light in you is darkness, how great is the darkness! No one can serve two masters; for a slave will either hate the one and love the other, or be devoted to the one and despise the other. You cannot serve God and wealth.'

If it were possible to sum up the whole teaching of Jesus about money and possessions in one short saying, it would certainly be, 'Where your treasure is, there your heart will be also.' In themselves, money and possessions are not evil, so long as we 'own' them. The trouble comes when they 'own' us. We can see that from the advice of Jesus to his disciples to use their 'wealth' wisely, as the 'children of this age' do (see Luke 16:8, 11).

Jesus had wealthy people among his followers, including women who supported him 'out of their resources' (Luke 8:3). Clearly they were wealthy people, but they used their wealth wisely. Yet on one occasion he insisted that a wealthy man who wished to follow him should sell all that he owned and distribute the money to the poor (Luke 18:22) and warned that 'it is easier for a camel to go through the eye of a needle than for someone who is rich to enter the kingdom of God' (Luke 18:25). And always there is this emphasis on the danger of putting our trust in riches. For Jesus, there was no question that pursuing wealth and possessions was a destructive course of action, a corruption of priorities and a way of life doomed to disappointment.

This is probably best illustrated in a short parable Jesus told, in answer to a man in the crowd who asked him to tell his brother to 'divide the family inheritance' with him. Jesus began his answer with a general statement of principle: 'Be on your guard against all kinds of greed; for one's life does not consist in the abundance of possessions.' He then told them a parable, to drive the point home—it's one we have looked at earlier, in considering 'Ambition and work'.

A rich man was doing very well—indeed, so well that his crops were overflowing the available storage space. He decided that the only answer was to embark on a programme of expansion. Then, the rich man reflected to himself, he would have made ample provision for his future comfort and security, and could sit back and enjoy things for the rest of his life—'relax, eat, drink and be merry'.

But God had other plans for him. 'You fool!' God said to him. 'This very night your life is being demanded of you. And the things you have prepared, whose will they be?' Jesus added a telling comment of his own: 'So it is with those who store up treasures for themselves but are not rich towards God' (see Luke 12:13–21).

Here we can see the heart of the teaching of Jesus about wealth. For him, true wealth was a matter of being 'rich towards God', of 'storing up for yourselves treasures in heaven'. Beside that absolute priority, everything else fades into insignificance. What use are possessions, subject to 'moth, rust and burglary'—and, we might add, inflation and the eccentricities of the stock market!—if we have no *eternal* security. And that kind of security simply cannot be bought. The truly 'rich' person may be a wealthy woman who uses her money to support the work of God, or in contrast a very poor widow who gave her last copper coins in the same cause (Mark 12:42). The size of their bank balances is not the determining factor, but the use they make of what God has given them.

In the end, money and possessions are, in the slightly dismissive word of Jesus, 'things'. They are neither permanent nor secure. To pin our hopes on them, to give our life's energy and commitment to pursuing them, is futile. No one can serve two masters, Jesus points out. 'You cannot serve God and wealth' (v. 24). In life, each of us must have one over-arching goal, the focus of our commitment. To make that goal 'wealth'—the Gospel word is Aramaic, *Mammon*—is to put our heart into a vacuum.

'Where your treasure is, there your heart will be also.' We all need a 'treasure', a precious thing that gives direction, meaning and pur-pose to life. Jesus urges his followers to choose a better treasure than money and a better goal than acquiring possessions. That 'better goal' is 'treasure in heaven'—something of lasting value, reflecting God's priorities of justice, mercy, generosity and love.

To REFLECT

In the context of modern life, what would constitute a 'wise' and Christian use of money and personal resources? How can we set ourselves higher goals in life, when money seems to run everything (and we certainly can't survive without it)?

Other passages you may wish to consult: Matthew 6:2–4; Matthew 22:15–22; Luke 12:13–21; Luke 16:10–13

OBEDIENCE

MATTHEW 21:28–32

'What do you think? A man had two sons; he went to the first and said, "Son, go and work in the vineyard today." He answered, "I will not"; but later he changed his mind and went. The father went to the second and said the same; and he answered, "I go, sir"; but he did not go. Which of the two did the will of his father?' They said, 'The first.' Jesus said to them, 'Truly I tell you, the tax collectors and the prostitutes are going into the kingdom of God ahead of you. For John came to you in the way of righteousness and you did not believe him, but the tax collectors and the prostitutes believed him; and even after you saw it, you did not change your minds and believe him.'

As so often, the heart of the teaching of Jesus on a particular subject is best caught in a story. That's certainly so with the tricky subject of 'obedience'—not a popular concept with modern people. I was brought up on the saying, 'Disobedience may seem fun, but it is a risk to run.' That was by my mother. The RAF added a sterner version of it: orders were to be *obeyed*, not discussed, argued about or questioned—and, yes, even wrong orders! I suppose those wretched robots, the Daleks, captured the modern idea of obedience, as they terrorized their victims with the metallic shriek, 'Obey! Obey!'

Yet today children are encouraged to discuss, to question, to argue —and I'm glad they are. The era of unquestioning obedience to authority probably ended with the death of the Soviet Union, following the earlier discrediting of a similarly authoritarian and unquestioned authority in Nazi Germany. The track record of unswerving obedience has not been a good one over the centuries, either.

So when one says that Jesus calls us to 'obey' the will of his Father, we may feel a qualm of misgiving. Isn't this that voice of authority— religious, in this case—which demands that people abandon restraint, reason, even humanity in submission to its ultimate and infallible demands?

This story puts the issue in a rather different context. A father asks two of his sons to go and work that day in his vineyard—a perfectly reasonable request of two young men who presumably shared the work of the farm. One said he would go, but didn't. The other said he wouldn't, but in the event did. Jesus' question is deceptively simple: 'Which of them did his father's will?' There were no prizes, of course, for getting the answer right.

The teaching of Jesus is always intensely practical. True religion, for him, is not a matter of words and ceremonies, but of day-to-day obedience to the will of his heavenly Father. After all, he is the king of the kingdom of heaven, and its subjects are bound together by the fact that they voluntarily submit to his rule. In the story of Adam and Eve, human beings were expelled from God's kingdom because they thought they knew better than their creator. Their sin was pride, leading to disobedience. Now, in the coming of Jesus, human beings are offered a way back into that kingdom by imitating his humble obedience to the will of God. So, in a sense, it is through the 'obedience' of Jesus that the 'disobedience' of the human race is to be removed—an argument rehearsed in his usual relentless way by Paul in Romans 5:18–19.

At any rate, Jesus put great store on the principle of obedience to the will of God. Indeed, it was the guiding principle of his whole life, and the example which he offered to his followers. It was no use chanting, 'Lord, Lord' if they were not prepared to do 'the will of my Father in heaven' (Matthew 7:21). That was the touchstone of discipleship: not what they said but what they did. So the 'chief priests and elders'—to whom these remarks are addressed—said all the right things but didn't do them, while the 'tax collectors and prostitutes' who followed Jesus were welcomed into the kingdom of heaven. And that, of course, is the point of the story about the two sons: the test is not words, but *doing what the Father requires*.

This is not at all the same thing as blind obedience to a superior power, because the one who issues the command is the 'heavenly Father'. That is a very significant title, one much loved by Jesus. It speaks of loving purpose rather than dominant will. The God who calls us to 'obey' is also the God who knows us perfectly, cares perfectly about our well-being and has a whole and perfect view of the context of our lives.

As so often, the letter of James provides a helpful application of the teaching of his brother, Jesus. He writes, 'Those who look into the perfect law, the law of liberty, and persevere, being not hearers who forget but doers who act—they will be blessed in their doing' (1:25). That captures the spirit of the teaching of Jesus beautifully. The 'law' of his heavenly Father is 'perfect'. More than that, it is a 'law of liberty', a law that does not restrict us as human beings, but sets us free. Of course, we have to 'hear' that law. We need to *listen* to the word of God. But then comes the test: not just hearing but 'doing'. And those who do not simply 'hear', but 'obey', will be 'blessed' (Luke 11:28).

To REFLECT

To obey someone who (a) loves you, (b) knows all about you and (c) desires only the best for you is not exactly irksome!

Other passages you may wish to consult: Matthew 7:21–23; Matthew 12:46–50; Luke 11:27, 28; Luke 17:10

Day 22 (Saturday)

Peace

LUKE 10:5, 6

'Whatever house you enter, first say, "Peace to this house!" And if anyone is there who shares in peace, your peace will rest on that person; but if not, it will return to you.'

MATTHEW 5:9

'Blessed are the peacemakers, for they will be called children of God.'

LUKE 8:48

'Daughter, your faith has made you well; go in peace.'

MATTHEW 26:52

Then Jesus said to him, 'Put your sword back into its place; for all who take the sword will perish by the sword.'

At the birth of Jesus the angels praised God for a double blessing: 'Glory to God in the highest heaven, and on earth peace among those whom he favours' (Luke 2:14). Yet in the event the coming of Jesus did not bring peace on earth. He recognized that fact himself: 'Do you think that I have come to bring peace to the earth? No, I tell you, but rather division!' (Luke 12:51) So we are immediately alerted to the idea that 'peace', for Jesus, is much more than merely absence of conflict.

The rather strange injunction to the seventy disciples whom he sent out ahead of him (see Luke 10:1) bears this out. The customary greeting among the Jews of our Lord's time (and indeed still in Israel today) was *shalom*, peace. So his disciples would have expected, without any special instructions from Jesus, to greet each household that they visited in that way. Jesus doesn't countermand that, but simply observes that peace will only rest on that person if they 'share in your peace'—literally, are a 'son of peace'. In other words, peace can never be one-sided; it involves 'sharing'. The disciples' message of peace must evoke a response of peace, otherwise its blessings will be withheld ('it will return to you').

So 'peace', for Jesus, is not an easy option, by any means. It is certainly not a matter of condoning evil or compromising principle. That is why the teaching of Jesus does not 'bring peace' of itself. By its challenge to conscience and will it inevitably provokes division, even between the members of a family. Yet if the response to his message is belief and acceptance, then the 'blessing' of peace ensues.

True peace is being 'well', being 'whole'. That was the peace with which Jesus sent away the woman who had come and touched him, seeking healing from a long-term haemorrhage (Luke 8:48). This peace is the reward of faith, because true, inner peace comes only when the turmoil of human anxiety and fear is replaced by trust in God. This was the 'peace' that Jesus offered the frightened disciples in the upper room after his resurrection (see Luke 24:36; John 20:21, 26). And it is a peace that is unaffected by external circumstances. It is a state of being at one with God, of being 'complete' in him, the fulfilment of what the New Testament calls 'salvation', being 'made whole'.

But Jesus lived in violent times, as we do. Revenge was a way of life in some quarters. There was a culture of violence induced, or at any rate nourished, by the humiliation of the Jewish people under Gentile conquerors. Many saw the sword and the knife as the only realistic answers to the plight of Israel.

It is against that background that Jesus exhorted his followers to 'love their enemies' (Matthew 5:44)—to most ears, a message of bizarre irrelevance. And it was in that context that he warned his closest friends against the dangers inherent in turning to violence as a solution to problems, even what would surely have been justifiable violence. When the temple guard came to arrest Jesus, one of his disciples, identified by John as the impetuous Peter, took a sword and struck one of the servants of the high priest, cutting off his ear. It was this action that provoked the clearest possible repudiation by Jesus of violence as an answer to violence: 'Those who take the sword will perish by the sword.' History has demonstrated the truth of his words over and over again, but the human race still finds it a very difficult lesson to learn.

So whether we are thinking of peace as a state of mind, or as the description of a society free from violence and bloodshed, the teaching of Jesus addresses the situation with its customary clarity and lack of ambiguity. For a society free from violence, we must renounce the use of force as a means of achieving even just ends. In the words of Isaiah—looking on to the messianic age of peace—we shall need to 'beat our swords into ploughshares, and our spears into pruning hooks' (Isaiah 2:4). This is not to condone evil, which must still be confronted and opposed, but it is to recognize the futility of vengeance.

And for a heart at peace, which is the deep and true meaning of *shalom*, we shall need to turn from our restless anxiety and find wholeness through faith in the God of peace.

To REFLECT

Jesus said that the 'peacemakers' would be called the 'children of God', presumably because they 'take after' their heavenly Father. But peacemaking has a price. It is seldom achieved without sacrifice. Jesus himself made peace for us 'through the blood of his cross' (Colossians 1:20). What sort of price are we prepared to pay for 'peace', both our own, and the peace of the society in which we live?

Other passages you may wish to consult: Matthew 10:34–39; Luke 19:41–44; John 16:33

FOURTH WEEK

in LENT

PAUSE *for* PRAYER

JOHN 9:4, 5

Jesus said, 'We must work the works of him who sent me while it is day; night is coming when no one can work. As long as I am in the world, I am the light of the world.'

We have seen during the past week how absolutely central to the ministry of Jesus was this conviction that he had been 'sent'. He did not act on his own, but as the agent and embodiment of the will and purpose of his Father, the one who had sent him into the world. All through his life he was driven by this vocation, which John's Gospel, especially, sees as his 'work'. On the night of his betrayal he was able to say to his Father that he had 'finished the work that you gave me to do' (17:4).

In this saying, Jesus is warning his disciples that the time is short. The 'night', the darkness that would enfold the world on Good Friday, was coming—and perhaps there is a hint here of that other 'darkness' that Jesus taught about in the synoptic Gospels, the darkness that would come upon the people when the Messiah had finally been rejected. But 'while I am in the world' there is light for the world.

Yet, as the Sermon on the Mount reminds us, that light *would* remain, in the disciples. 'You (plural: you disciples) are the light of the world … Let your light shine before others' (Matthew 5:14, 16). The unique light for the world that was the incarnate Son of God can continue to shine in the world that he 'visited' long ago, but only if his followers *reflect* it.

A PRAYER

May the light of Christ, the light of the world, illuminate my life,
And may his light, reflected in me, shine before others,
So that they may give glory to the Father of lights.

POVERTY

LUKE 6:20-26

Then he looked up at his disciples and said: 'Blessed are you who are poor, for yours is the kingdom of God. Blessed are you who are hungry now, for you will be filled. Blessed are you who weep now, for you will laugh. Blessed are you when people hate you, and when they exclude you, revile you, and defame you on account of the Son of Man. Rejoice in that day and leap for joy, for surely your reward is great in heaven; for that is what their ancestors did to the prophets. But woe to you who are rich, for you have received your consolation. Woe to you who are full now, for you will be hungry. Woe to you who are laughing now, for you will mourn and weep. Woe to you when all speak well of you, for that is what their ancestors did to the false prophets.'

There can be no doubt that Jesus felt a special affinity with poor people, possibly because he came from a poor family himself. All of these terms are relative, of course. By modern western standards, almost everybody in the Galilee and Judea of Jesus' time was poor, except for the grotesquely wealthy members of the royal or priestly households. There were wealthy landowners, of course (some described in unflattering terms in the Gospels), and the so-called 'tax collectors' were able to line their pockets at the expense of the ordinary people. But most people were poor, in the sense that they had no reserves or savings and depended on harvests (of land or sea) to meet their daily needs. The prayer for the provision of 'bread enough for the day', which is probably the literal meaning of the petition in the Lord's Prayer, would have had immense relevance to most of those who listened to the teaching of Jesus.

He described his message as 'good news for poor people' (Luke 4:18), and it is obvious that his mass audiences were largely made up of what the Authorized Version rather quaintly calls 'common people' (Mark 12:37). His chief opponents were the powerful leaders of church and state, and his most damning indictments were of the perils of power and wealth. Conversely, he seems to have taught that poverty itself, far from being a curse, could—if properly regarded—be a blessing.

So it is significant that in both the lists of 'blessings' in the Gospels—the so-called 'Beatitudes' in Matthew and Luke—the first 'blessing' is on the 'poor'. In the passage above, Luke's version, it is very stark: 'Blessed are you who are poor.' Matthew has 'blessed are the poor *in spirit*', though the meaning is probably identical. In neither case is it simply a matter of saying that those who have nothing, in terms of possessions, are 'happy'. That would be a ridiculous suggestion, like the proposal that those who starve are happy, or those whose children have no clothes.

But the fact that 'the poor' head the list of those who are blessed in both Gospels places that condition in a special place. We might well read both lists as expansions of the idea that poverty is the key to blessedness: those who weep, those who are hated, those who are excluded, reviled and abused are also 'poor', in this sense. They have no strength of their own, no sense of independence. They are under no illusion that they are masters of their own fate, or in charge of their destiny. They know that their survival depends on others rather than themselves.

And, in a strange way, that *is* the key to blessedness. The problem for those who are rich, or 'full', or 'laughing' is that they have no need of others. They have lost the sense of dependence which is the very heart of faith. They have built their lives on a basis of self-sufficiency, whereas the whole teaching of Jesus is that the happy life is built on the sufficiency of God. The rich are not excluded from the kingdom of God because they are rich, but because their riches have blinded them to their need of him. Somewhere behind all this lurks the objection of the modern mind: religion is just a crutch for the weak. Exactly. But in the sight of our Maker we are *all* weak, *all* dependent on his grace, *all* in need of forgiveness, mercy and divine guidance.

All through the ministry of Jesus, the 'poor' figure prominently. They heard him gladly. They came to him for fish and bread, and followed in the hope of a permanent supply of free food (see Luke 9:12–17 and compare John 6:26, 34). They brought their relatives and friends to him for healing. They hung on his words, because no one had ever spoken to them like this before, or treated them with such respect. It was the 'ordinary' people who gathered to him in their thousands, and the ordinary people of Galilee who followed him to Jerusalem at the end.

Yet in this emphasis on the worthiness of the poor and the intrinsic 'value' of poverty, Jesus was picking up a great theme of the Hebrew scriptures. All through the teaching of the Law runs the command to care for the poor, who are to be given respect and consideration (see, for example, Exodus 23:3). And the Psalms echo again and again God's special love and concern for the poor among his creatures: 'The poor will eat and be satisfied'; 'He raises the poor from the dust'; 'The Lord secures justice for the poor'. It is not that God 'approves' of people being poor, or connives at their deprivation. Far from it. He has good news for the poor, and his Son is the bringer of it.

To REFLECT

Francis of Assisi felt that poverty was part of discipleship. Still today the witness of Franciscans is to the value of a 'modest lifestyle', to ensure that money and possessions do not blind us to the true values. How can modern Christians find this 'poverty of spirit' which will enable them to 'see God'?

Other passages you may wish to consult: Matthew 19:23–26; Luke 6:24, 25; Luke 9:3; Luke 14:12–14; Luke 16:19–31

PRAYER

LUKE 11:2-13

He said to them, 'When you pray, say: Father, hallowed be your name. Your kingdom come. Give us each day our daily bread. And forgive us our sins, for we ourselves forgive everyone indebted to us. And do not bring us to the time of trial.' And he said to them, 'Suppose one of you has a friend, and you go to him at midnight and say to him, "Friend, lend me three loaves of bread; for a friend of mine has arrived, and I have nothing to set before him." And he answers from within, "Do not bother me; the door has already been locked, and my children are with me in bed; I cannot get up and give you anything." I tell you, even though he will not get up and give him anything because he is his friend, at least because of his persistence he will get up and give him whatever he needs. So I say to you, Ask, and it will be given to you; search, and you will find; knock, and the door will be opened for you. For everyone who asks receives, and everyone who searches finds, and for everyone who knocks, the door will be opened. Is there anyone among you who, if your child asks for a fish, will give a snake instead of a fish? Or if the child asks for an egg, will give a scorpion? If you then, who are evil, know how to give good gifts to your children, how much more will the heavenly Father give the Holy Spirit to those who ask him!'

Jesus prayed, frequently and passionately; and he often spoke about prayer to his followers and to the crowds. Yet it's hard to find in his teaching answers to the questions modern people most often ask about prayer. The passage above is in answer to the request from his disciples to teach them *how* to pray. A comparable group of people today would ask *why* they should pray—and why, when we do pray, our prayers seem to go unanswered.

Prayer was simply part of the life of the world in the time of Jesus. Jews prayed in temple, synagogue and home to the God of Abraham, Isaac and Jacob. Gentiles prayed in temple, shrine and grove—and at the altars of their household gods—to the deities of their own religions. Not to pray would have been to provoke divine displeasure, at the very least. To pray was to invoke divine assistance—to put it crudely, to get God or the gods to do what the petitioner wanted. A good harvest, victory over enemies, healing from disease or an assured place in the life beyond: these were the endless topics of prayer in what was an age of prayer. But the agenda of Jesus on the subject of prayer was much more radical. For him, the heart of prayer was the first petition in the 'formula' that he gave to his disciples: 'Your kingdom come.' In Matthew's version it is expanded by the interpretative phrase, 'Your will be done on earth, as it is in heaven.' That defines prayer as *co-operation in the will of God*. Far from being a way of getting God to do what *we* want, it is a way of involvement in what *God* wants. Thus it becomes a 'kingdom' prayer—a prayer that has as its goal the truth, mercy, love and justice of God.

The story that follows the Lord's Prayer here might easily be taken as implying that the way to get what we want (in prayer, or in life) is by sheer persistence, by nagging a reluctant giver into handing over the 'bread'. This could be (and sometimes is) applied to prayer, as though our sheer persistence will eventually wring from God what he is reluctant to give us. But in fact the point of the story lies in the tell-tale phrase 'how much more' (v. 13). If the reluctant neighbour eventually hands over the loaves, and fallible and flawed parents know how to give good things to their children, *how much more* will God gladly and generously give 'good gifts' to those who ask him? It is a parable of contrast. God is *not* like the neighbour, and he is *more generous* than even the best human parent. So how can we doubt that he hears our prayers and through them works for our good? Much the same point is made in the rather similar story of the widow and the unjust judge (Luke 18:3–8).

But we must notice what that 'good' is, and here Luke provides a revealing expansion of Matthew's 'good things'. The gift that God gladly gives those who ask him is 'the Holy Spirit'—nothing less. Not the lottery jackpot, or a new house, or even good health, but the most precious gift God has, his own life-giving presence. The gift is to those who 'ask', 'search' and 'knock', but who do so in search of that 'good gift', not some private desire.

This raises the question, how are we to know if we are praying in line with the will of God? The answer is that we don't, and can't. Even Jesus in his prayers recognized that. In the Garden of Gethsemane on the night of his betrayal he prayed that he might be spared the cup of suffering '*if* you (the Father) are willing', following that petition with a recommitment to his Father's purpose: 'Yet, not my will but yours be done' (see Luke 22:42). If Jesus in his prayers needed to 'explore' the will of God, we may be sure that we shall need to.

But that should not prevent us from praying—simply sharing with God, as Jesus did, the longing and fears of our heart. Provided we understand the over-arching principle of his will, we may ask for anything, safe in the knowledge that what we receive will be the best for us. This, it would seem, is what John's Gospel refers to as praying 'in my name' (14:14).

There are two other matters of principle in the teaching of Jesus on prayer which must be mentioned. The first is the practice of gratitude. Prayer is not simply about asking, even for the Holy Spirit, but about expressing our thanks to God for his generous love. Of ten lepers who came to Christ seeking healing, all of whom received it, only one paused to give thanks (Luke 17:15–19). For that, he was given a special blessing. The other principle lies behind the whole idea of prayer. Why, if God knows what is best and has the power to do it, is there any need for a human intercessor? Why doesn't he just do it? It's a very modern question! Yet the everyday experience of parents and grandparents should give us the answer. In the process of asking, giving, receiving, thanking, a vital process of bonding goes on. The giver is able to show love and care, the recipient can practise gratitude, and both are brought closer together in a parent–child relationship of dependence, trust and mutual love. It is a lovely 'secret', which the disciple can discover only by constant practice!

To REFLECT

'When you pray, say "Father"...' One of the distinctive things about the prayers of Jesus is the use of the intimate form of the word for Father, Abba. To know that we bring our needs to one who created us and loves us makes all the difference.

Other passages you may wish to consult: Matthew 6:5–13; Matthew 7:7–11; Matthew 26:39–42; Luke 18:1–8; John 14:11–14

PRIORITIES

LUKE 12:29–34

'And do not keep striving for what you are to eat and what you are to drink, and do not keep worrying. For it is the nations of the world that strive after all these things, and your Father knows that you need them. Instead, strive for his kingdom, and these things will be given to you as well. Do not be afraid, little flock, for it is your Father's good pleasure to give you the kingdom. Sell your possessions, and give alms. Make purses for yourselves that do not wear out, an unfailing treasure in heaven, where no thief comes near and no moth destroys. For where your treasure is, there your heart will be also.'

This passage puts into memorable and vivid words an idea that recurs over and over again in the teaching of Jesus—the question of human priorities. He expressed it in story and sermon, and modelled it in his own life. The security of the believer is in 'the Father's good pleasure', and the Father's good pleasure is to 'give you the kingdom'. It is a marvellous and rewarding promise.

As we have seen, the 'kingdom of heaven' or the 'kingdom of God' is a central principle of the mission of Jesus. It is possible to live our lives under a new regime, one of love, justice and righteousness, where God's will is done. It is the ultimate state of blessedness, the only place of true happiness and human fulfilment. And it is offered now to those who will 'repent' and 'believe in the good news' (Mark 1:15). Sometimes in the synoptic Gospels, and almost always in John's Gospel, this state is described as 'eternal life' (see, for example, Luke 18:30 and John 3:16). 'Eternal life' is life in the kingdom of heaven, both now, imperfectly on earth, and eventually, perfectly, in heaven (where God's will is already perfectly done—Matthew 6:10). To receive the gift of eternal life, or to live in the 'kingdom of heaven' are, then, virtually the same thing. And it is the Father's 'good pleasure'—what a glorious phrase!—to give it to his 'little flock'.

To seek this blessing is the disciple's priority. 'Strive *first* for the kingdom of God,' said Jesus, and 'all these things' (food, clothing, health, peace of mind) shall be yours as well (Matthew 6:33). For this, the disciple should be prepared to lose 'the whole world' (Mark 8:36). For this, all earthly ties and worldly considerations are to be set aside, if necessary (see Luke 9:57–62), because 'no one who puts a hand to the plough and looks back is fit for the kingdom of God'.

The point is powerfully made in several parables. The 'kingdom of heaven' is like treasure buried in a field. The one who finds it is prepared to sell all that he has in order to buy the field and acquire the treasure. Or it is like a merchant in search of fine pearls, who is willing to sell all the run-of-the-mill pearls he owns in order to possess the one 'pearl of great value' (Matthew 13:44–46). The kingdom of heaven, quite simply, is the most valuable thing in the whole world, and no price is too great to pay in order to be part of it.

Yet it is a gift! 'It is your Father's good pleasure to *give* you the kingdom'! This priceless possession is for the 'little flock', the *microi*, the despised ones, the people of no power and influence, the blessed poor who were so dear to the heart of Jesus. 'Do not be afraid!' Why should they? The greatest thing in the world is theirs, a gift that will last beyond the fading glamour and tawdry wealth of those who at present oppress them.

It can never have been put in more telling words than these: 'Do not store up for yourselves treasures on earth, where moth and rust consume and where thieves break in and steal; but store up for yourselves treasures in heaven, where neither moth nor rust consumes and where thieves do not break in and steal. For where your treasure is, there your heart will be also' (Matthew 6:19–21). There is the clear-cut priority, and the test of its fulfilment is the desire of our hearts. In the end, we get what we truly want more than anything else, and truly to long for God and the righteousness of his kingdom is the only goal of absolute and eternal value.

The good news of the kingdom, said Jesus, is like good seed sown in a field. It has the potential to grow into a wonderful harvest, but there are many influences at work in the world which can stunt its growth. Among them are 'the cares of the world, and the lure of wealth, and the desire for other things' (Mark 4:19). One is tempted to say, little changes! 'Things' still stand like 'thorns', choking the good seed of the gospel, instant and attractive, colourful and desirable—but of no value beyond the present. 'Treasure in heaven', 'the kingdom', 'eternal life' are God's special offers to his 'little flock'. It is folly on the grand scale to lose them for the sake of a few consumer durables and a bit of neighbourly admiration.

To REFLECT

Are my priorities the priorities of the kingdom of heaven,
or of the 'kingdoms of this world'?

Other passages you may wish to consult: Matthew 18:1–4; Mark 8:36, 37; Luke 4:4; Luke 10:38–42; Luke 12:33, 34; Luke 18:29, 30

DAY 26 (THURSDAY)

PURPOSE *of* LIFE

MATTHEW 5:13–16

'You are the salt of the earth; but if salt has lost its taste, how can its saltiness be restored? It is no longer good for anything, but is thrown out and trampled under foot. You are the light of the world. A city built on a hill cannot be hid. No one after lighting a lamp puts it under the bushel basket, but on the lampstand, and it gives light to all in the house. In the same way, let your light shine before others, so that they may see your good works and give glory to your Father in heaven.'

For the most succinct answer to the question, 'What is the purpose of life?' one would have to turn to John's Gospel. 'This is eternal life, that they may know you, the only true God, and Jesus Christ whom you have sent' (17:3). That is not, of course, the language of the synoptic Gospels, for the most part, yet there is an intriguing exception. It is known to biblical scholars as the 'Johannine thunderbolt', because suddenly, right in the middle of both Matthew's and Luke's Gospels, come these words from the lips of Jesus: 'All things have been handed over to me by my Father; and no one knows the Son except the Father, and no one knows the Father except the Son and anyone to whom the Son chooses to reveal him' (Matthew 11:27; compare Luke 10:22). There is the unmistakable 'style' of the Jesus of the fourth Gospel, claiming that true 'knowledge' of God is only available through 'the Son', and those to whom the Son 'chooses to reveal him'. So in the whole Gospel record there is a unanimous message: to know God is the 'chief end' of humanity, and it is through Jesus Christ alone that he can be fully known. The purpose of life is to know God.

But if that is the great goal, then what are its particulars? For many people, 'knowing God' is an elusive, even nebulous kind of idea. One would expect Jesus the teacher to flesh it out in terms that ordinary people can understand and respond to. And that is, of course, exactly what he does.

Here, in these well-known words, the great goal is expressed in two contrasting particulars. These words are, of course, part of the Sermon on the Mount, which was addressed not to the 'crowds' but to 'his disciples' (see Matthew 5:1). They are the citizens of the new kingdom, the kingdom of God, and Jesus is now setting out for them what life to kingdom standards means. Those who want to 'know God' must, of necessity, be members of that kingdom, or how can they hope to see the king?

And the members of that kingdom are called to be both 'salt' and 'light'—two contrasting roles. Salt, in the ancient world, had two uses. Firstly, and most importantly, it was a preservative. Before the days of refrigeration, salt was the only way to keep meat, for instance, from going bad during the months when it was not naturally available. Salt kept corruption at bay. Salt inhibited the advance of decay.

Secondly, salt (as it does still today) brought the full flavour out of things, turning what was otherwise bland and insipid into a delight for the palate.

The disciples of Jesus, the people of the kingdom, were to fulfil both of those functions in the world. They would hold back by their witness and life the advance of corruption and decay in society. And they would bring flavour and zest into lives which without them would be bland. The kingdom spelt colour, life, hope, imagination, beauty—and they were the 'salt' that would release those gifts of God into the world.

At the same time, they were to be 'light'—indeed, 'the light of the world'. In John's Gospel Jesus calls himself 'the light of the world' (John 8:12), but his followers were called to reflect that divine light into their surroundings. Light shows up what is evil; light dispels darkness; light brings hope and encouragement; light reveals the safe path. In all of those ways the disciples were to be light. It was their calling, an outworking of the great goal of knowing God. They were not to 'know God', in other words, in a selfish, private, little cocoon of piety. They were to know God and represent him, as salt and light, in the world in which he had put them.

When Jesus called his first disciples it was with a rather odd invitation: 'Follow me and I will make you fish for people' (Mark 1:17). I don't think he was saying that their sole calling as his followers was to 'catch' other people and bring them into his kingdom, though that idea is certainly contained in his words. What he was saying, surely, was that if they followed him he would give them new goals, far greater than running a little fishing business on the banks of Galilee. 'Follow me, and I will transform your life… follow me, and nothing will be the same again… follow me, and you will bring light to dark places and the joy of life to those who live empty lives.' Follow me, in other words, and you will 'know God', and share him with others.

To REFLECT

We all need goals in life, the feeling that it's going somewhere, that it has purpose and meaning. How can this teaching of Jesus help me to set my sights on the 'great goal' and on the particular goals which will make it real for me?

Other passages you may wish to consult: Matthew 5:48; Matthew 11:27, 28; Luke 4:18,19; Luke 10:20

REPENTANCE

LUKE 24:44–48

Then he said to them, 'These are my words that I spoke to you
while I was still with you—that everything written about me in the
law of Moses, the prophets, and the psalms must be fulfilled.'
Then he opened their minds to understand the scriptures, and he
said to them, 'Thus it is written, that the Messiah is to suffer and
to rise from the dead on the third day, and that repentance and
forgiveness of sins is to be proclaimed in his name to all nations,
beginning from Jerusalem. You are witnesses of these things.'

We don't have much record of the teaching that Jesus gave to his
disciples after his resurrection, apart from tantalizing hints in his discourse with Cleopas and his partner on the road to Emmaus, and his
words of recommissioning to Peter. But here we have a summary
of what we might call the 'post-resurrection' gospel of Jesus, the
message that his followers were to take to the whole world. It is so
brief as to be instantly memorable: 'repentance and forgiveness of
sins in the name of Jesus'.

On the day of Pentecost we find Peter being faithful to this
message: 'Repent, and be baptized every one of you in the name of
Jesus Christ so that your sins may be forgiven' (Acts 2:38). The
disciples here, in the upper room, were told to 'stay here... until you
have been clothed with power from on high'. On the day of
Pentecost, after the outpouring of the Spirit, there was no longer any
need to wait: 'You will receive the gift of the Holy Spirit.'

Yet this post-resurrection message was not entirely new. Indeed,
right from the start of the ministry of Jesus, his call was to 'repent and
believe', and the consequence of that repentance was the forgiveness
of sins. When Jesus first came into Galilee 'proclaiming the good
news of God' his call was direct and simple: 'Repent, and believe the
good news.' From then on, repentance and faith were the two keys to
his blessing. It was the self-righteous who shut themselves off from it
by their reluctance to repent, even when confronted with his works

of power. The little lakeside towns of Chorazin, Bethsaida and Capernaum, the scenes of his greatest miracles, would be 'brought down to Hades' because they had not responded with repentance. By comparison, he said, those bywords for evil, Tyre, Sidon and Sodom, would have 'repented long ago in sackcloth and ashes' if faced with the same evidence. Repentance was the key, not outward profession of religious belief.

The word 'repentance' has not had a happy history. It conveys to most people a grim obsession with 'sin' and the need to 'grovel' before God for our misdeeds. In fact, as Jesus uses it, it is a very positive word, expressing a desire for a fresh start. The Greek word *metanoia* literally means a 'change of mind', a total reversal of attitude. That was what Jesus longed to see—an admission that God is right and we are wrong, that arguing our innocence is a lost cause, but frankly admitting our failure is the first, vital step to forgiveness and a new start.

Nowhere is the point made more tellingly than in Jesus's story of the two men who went up to the temple to pray. One was a Pharisee, who began his prayers by reciting his acts of piety: 'God, I thank you that I am not like other people… I fast twice a week; I give a tenth of all my income…' The other man was a tax collector, which is short-hand in the Gospels for a swindling traitor to the nation, one who would work for the occupying power and plunder the poor for taxes over and above the set amounts. He stood far off, would not even look up to heaven, but beat his breast, saying, 'God, be merciful to me, a sinner!' The judgment of Jesus is unambiguous: 'I tell you, this man (the tax collector) went down to his house justified rather than the other; for all who exalt themselves will be humbled, but all who humble themselves will be exalted' (Luke 18:11–14).

Jesus described his ministry in terms of a personal mission to the repentant. 'Those who are well have no need of a physician, but those who are sick; I have come to call not the righteous but sinners to repentance' (Luke 5:31, 32). These words were addressed to a group of 'Pharisees and their scribes', men who definitely did not think of themselves as 'sinners', but as 'righteous' people. Jesus had nothing to offer them, because they thought that they needed nothing.

'Repentance' was the great message of John the Baptist, of course. It was, and is, a process of turning from one attitude of mind to another, and is an indispensable element of true conversion. Jesus picked up the same theme, but invariably connected it with a positive step of faith: 'repent *and believe.*' Those are the two great gospel imperatives, intimately linked with the forgiveness of sins for which Christ gave his life. It's a testimony to the unity of God's purpose that the first and last commands of the incarnate Jesus linked those two imperatives together, at the first, for the people of Galilee, and at the last for 'all nations'.

To REFLECT

It's wrong to think of repentance as something miserable and demeaning. Jesus saw it as an occasion of joy—joy for the one who has repented, and 'joy in heaven' (Luke 15:7, 10). Indeed, it's like finding lost treasure! (Luke 15:9)

Other passages you may wish to consult: Matthew 4:17; Matthew 11:20–24; Luke 15:1–31

RESURRECTION & LIFE
after DEATH

MATTHEW 22:29–33

*Jesus answered them, 'You are wrong, because you know neither
the scriptures nor the power of God. For in the resurrection they
neither marry nor are given in marriage, but are like angels in
heaven. And as for the resurrection of the dead, have you not read
what was said to you by God, "I am the God of Abraham, the God
of Isaac, and the God of Jacob"? He is God not of the dead, but of
the living.' And when the crowd heard it, they were astounded
at his teaching.*

These words of Jesus are his reply to a long and involved question
put to him by some Sadducees, and in themselves they constitute
the strongest and clearest instance of the teaching of Jesus about
the resurrection of individual human beings. His own resurrection
from the dead, strongly foretold in his own teaching (see, for
instance, Mark 8:31; 9:31; 10:34), while in a different category from
a 'general' resurrection, was the proof that God could raise the dead.
Here, however, Jesus is dealing with a much wider issue, and one
which was clearly a point of contention in the Judaism of his day: is
there life beyond death, or, as the Sadducees taught, does the soul
perish along with the body?

Their question was expressed as an actual case, though we may
assume it was a hypothetical one! It involved seven brothers, each
of whom, in obedience to the levirate law, in turn was married to
the same woman. This law, still current, it would seem, in the time
of Christ, required a man to marry his own brother's childless
widow and thus 'raise up' children for him. For the Sadducees this
continuity of birth was the only 'resurrection' that they recognized. In
the case that they put to Jesus, all seven brothers eventually died, and
so did the widow. The question then was, whose wife would she be
in the 'resurrection'? It was a hypocritical question, of course,

because they didn't believe there was going to be a resurrection at all. But they hoped that this example of legal absurdity would discredit the whole idea of life beyond death.

Jesus challenged their arguments on two grounds. The first was their very 'secular' concept of the resurrection life, as though it were simply a 'second innings' of the present one, lived out in identical fashion but in a different place. This showed their failure to grasp the true meaning of 'the scriptures' (v. 29)—the *whole* of the Hebrew scriptures, that is, rather than just the Pentateuch, which the Sadducees insisted was the only valid source of authority. This meant that they ignored such passages as Daniel 12:2: 'Many of those who sleep in the dust of the earth shall awake, some to everlasting life, and some to shame and everlasting contempt.'

'Everlasting life' is life lived in the power of God and is a whole new kind of life, literally beyond our comprehension. The apostle Paul sets out the position with great clarity in 1 Corinthians 15:35–50. We are to think of a 'new creation', not a re-run of the present order of things. Hence, questions about who would be married to whom, and whether people would be able to raise children in the life hereafter, are totally irrelevant, and even slightly ridiculous. The life of the resurrection is like the life of the 'angels'—a sharing in the life of God, where exclusivity, jealousy and possessiveness would have no place. Of course, loving relationships would continue and indeed reach their fulfilment, but in heaven disputes over the 'possession' of a partner would be unthinkable.

That is the first part of the argument of Jesus, a refutation of the Sadducees from the standpoint of the whole of the Hebrew scriptures. But then Jesus narrows his sights, as it were, and demolishes the Sadducees' argument from the authority of the part of the scriptures that they did recognize, the Pentateuch. He refers them to Exodus 3:6—Moses at the burning bush, a formative moment in the history of Israel. God would reveal to Moses his 'name', that's to say, his nature: *Yahweh*, 'I am who I am' (Exodus 3:14–16). He is a God of the present tense, a God who is constantly active and present in his creation, a God who lives, saves and keeps his promises. Yet he describes himself to Moses as the 'God of Abraham, Isaac and Jacob', who were at that time long dead. As R.T. France observes in his commentary on Matthew's Gospel, '"To be the God of" implies a caring, protecting relationship which is as permanent as the living God who makes it.' The great New Testament scholar J. Jeremias comments, 'With unsurpassable brevity this sentence says that faith in God includes the certainty of conquering death.'

That 'certainty' was demonstrated and confirmed in the resurrection of Jesus himself. It tells us that the 'kingdom of heaven', so central to his message, and its collateral gift, eternal life, are not optional extras to his teaching. They are at its heart, and at the heart of the purpose of his Father.

To REFLECT

Jesus did not simply talk about resurrection. He lived on earth the life of eternity—its values, insights, priorities and beauty.

Other passages you may wish to consult: Luke 7:11–17; Luke 24:36–49; John 11:23–27

FIFTH WEEK

in LENT

Pause *for* Prayer

John 11:33–35

When Jesus saw her weeping, and the Jews who came with her also weeping, he was greatly disturbed in spirit and deeply moved. He said, 'Where have you laid him?' They said to him, 'Lord, come and see.' Jesus began to weep.

As we saw yesterday, Jesus clearly believed, and taught vigorously, that there is life beyond death. Earlier in this same story (the raising of Lazarus) he had assured Martha, the sister of Lazarus, that her brother would 'rise again' (v. 23). Yet—and it *is* a mystery—Jesus was deeply moved at the tomb of his friend, 'disturbed in spirit', emotionally upset by the sight of the tears of the bystanders and Mary and Martha. 'Jesus began to weep.'

He knew that Lazarus would 'rise again'. But he knew, even more than that, that in a few moments the body of Lazarus would emerge from the tomb, fully alive again. So, *why weep*?

There are several possible answers, most of which involve the delicate balance of the human and divine in Jesus. As the Son of God he could speak of himself as the 'resurrection and the life' (v. 25). But as the Son of Man, born of Mary, knowing all the frailty and fears of our mortality, and the sorrow that death inevitably brings, he could be 'greatly disturbed' by the presence of death (v. 38). This little incident tells us much about the meaning of the incarnation. At God's right hand (in the imagery of the Bible) sits one who has been where we are, felt what we have felt, wept where we have wept. That's what it means to have a 'Saviour'.

A Prayer

Lord, you suffered for us, and you understand human suffering. Save us, and help us.

RIGHTEOUSNESS

MATTHEW 13:41–43

'The Son of Man will send his angels, and they will collect out of his kingdom all causes of sin and all evildoers, and they will throw them into the furnace of fire, where there will be weeping and gnashing of teeth. Then the righteous will shine like the sun in the kingdom of their Father. Let anyone with ears listen!'

'Righteous' and 'righteousness' are words that fall awkwardly on modern ears. On the whole, we are sceptical of 'righteousness': 'Oh, don't be so *righteous!*' And the most familiar use of the word is probably with the unpleasant prefix 'self': '*self*-righteous'. Yet it's one of the most common words in the synoptic Gospels, especially in Matthew, and almost always on the lips of Jesus.

Strangely enough, he used it as a word of both praise and rebuke. There's little doubt that sometimes when Jesus referred to the 'righteous' he meant the 'self-righteous', who felt that they needed no repentance (see, for instance, Mark 2:17 and Luke 15:7). I'm sure that the Pharisees would have seen themselves as 'righteous', and despised the 'unrighteous' tax collectors and prostitutes who gathered around Jesus.

But the most usual meaning of the word is clearly positive. After all, the final tribute to Jesus in Luke's Gospel, from the lips of the centurion who supervised his crucifixion, was that he was a 'righteous man' (Luke 23:47, NIV). It was the 'righteous' who fed the hungry, clothed the naked and visited those in prison (Matthew 25:37). To be truly 'righteous' is to be right with God, living the life God requires, following his commandments not only in letter but in spirit.

In fact, the true fulfilment of the Law is the hallmark of righteousness. To keep the Law of God in spirit as well as letter, in the way Jesus sets out in the Sermon on the Mount, is to have a 'righteousness' which 'exceeds that of the scribes and Pharisees' (Matthew

5:20)—and without such righteousness, Jesus warns, 'you will never enter the kingdom of heaven'.

So 'righteousness' is important, indeed central, to being a disciple of Jesus and a citizen of the kingdom. Yet the teaching of Jesus constantly emphasizes that this righteousness is much more than obedience to a code of rules or observance of a set of ritual acts. It is about a clean heart.

The passage quoted at the head of this chapter is a case in point. Jesus has been explaining to his disciples the parable of the 'weeds of the field', which was about the undeniable fact that there is evil present in the world, even though the world has been created by a good and holy God. 'An enemy' has planted weeds in his field (13:25) and they are now growing actively alongside the good seed. Rather than risk uprooting the 'wheat' by pulling up the weeds, both are to be allowed to 'grow together until the harvest' (v. 30). But then there will be a separation. The weeds will be collected and burned, and the wheat will be gathered into the barn. These words of Jesus are his commentary on the parable. At 'the end of the age' (v. 40) there will be an act of separation, by which God's kingdom will be cleansed of 'all causes of sin and all evildoers'. A day will come when God's creation will be delivered from the evil that has corrupted it and will become what God had intended it to be before the work of the 'enemy'. The fire will cleanse. 'There will be weeping and gnashing of teeth.'

It is too easy to shy away from this element in the teaching of Jesus. He clearly believed and taught that the evil which had infiltrated his Father's world would one day be eliminated. When that had taken place, then—and only then—'the righteous will shine like the sun in the kingdom of their Father'. The same Jesus who welcomed sinners and ate with them, the man who forgave the woman taken in adultery and those who crucified him, could speak with authority of a time when evil and injustice would be finally judged and the world purged for ever of their malign influence. He called his followers to 'hunger and thirst for righteousness' (Matthew 5:6) and to 'strive first for (God's) righteousness' (6:33). Only in that way could they be part of God's great purpose of eliminating evil from the world he had made and loved.

'Righteous' and 'righteousness' come from the Greek word *dikaios*, which means 'just, equitable, fair'. The word is closely connected with the idea of justice, with what is fit and proper, honest and upright. Jesus recognized that fallen human nature would struggle to meet God's requirement of moral perfection, so he taught the principle of repentance and forgiveness of sins. Those who can't be 'righteous' can be forgiven (Mark 2:17), and thus counted among the 'righteous ones' who will one day 'shine like the sun'. If that were not so, then there would be no 'good news of the kingdom', and no citizens of it, either.

To REFLECT

If God were to tolerate the presence of evil in his creation he would not be good. If he were to condemn all who have sinned he would not be merciful. The way of repentance that Jesus taught is the way of mercy and justice. No other way meets the requirements of a holy God and the desperate needs of a sinful humanity. This is the only true path to righteousness.

Other passages you may wish to consult: Matthew 3:15; Matthew 5:48; Matthew 7:12; Luke 18:9–14

DAY 30 (TUESDAY)

SACRIFICE

MATTHEW 19:27–30

*Then Peter said in reply, 'Look, we have left everything and
followed you. What then will we have?' Jesus said to them, 'Truly
I tell you, at the renewal of all things, when the Son of Man is
seated on the throne of his glory, you who have followed me will
also sit on twelve thrones, judging the twelve tribes of Israel. And
everyone who has left houses or brothers or sisters or father or
mother or children or fields, for my name's sake, will receive a
hundredfold, and will inherit eternal life. But many who are first
will be last, and the last will be first.'*

Jesus was not one to minimize the possible cost of following him.
Several times he warned would-be disciples that it would not be easy:
sacrifices would be called for. So 'no one who puts a hand to the
plough and looks back is fit for the kingdom of God' (Luke 9:62).
That warning followed a succession of half-hearted potential disciples,
who were deterred by family ties or the likelihood of physical hardship
('the Son of Man has nowhere to lay his head', 9:58).

When the mission of Jesus was riding high, and 'large crowds' were
travelling with him, Jesus seemed to go out of his way to discourage
them. 'Whoever comes to me and does not hate father and mother,
wife and children, brothers and sisters, yes, and even life itself,
cannot be my disciple' (Luke 14:25–27). The word 'hate' there is not
meant to be taken literally, in the sense of rejecting them or treating
them with repugnance. After all, while he was hanging on the cross
Jesus himself made careful and loving provision for his mother's
future. That hardly suggests 'hatred'! But, as we have seen, Jesus used
this language of extremes to drive home his message: not even the
closest human ties, sanctified by God's law itself, should stand
between the disciple and the demands of the kingdom. Christianity
does demand, and has always demanded, sacrifice. In Dietrich
Bonhoeffer's telling phrase, there is no such thing as 'cheap grace'.

I'm reminded of the story of the young Christian man who was enthusing to his battle-scarred Scottish Presbyterian minister about the joys of the Christian life. 'It's wonderful!' he said. 'One moment of blessing after another!' 'Ay, lad,' the minister responded, 'but it's a sore fight to the end.' I think Jesus would have said that both of them were right. As we can see in the passage at the head of this chapter, the blessing for the disciple is a hundred times better than anything he or she could have known outside the kingdom… and on top of that there is eternal life! Yet there is also the price to be paid, which may involve family, home, land, prosperity. Those who set out on the journey, Jesus would say, must first weigh the cost.

He drives that point home in a series of homely illustrations. A person wanting to build a tower sits down and estimates the cost, to see whether he will ever be in a position to complete it. A ruler about to engage in a military campaign first of all sits down and works out whether he has enough soldiers to overcome the enemy. Similarly, says Jesus, my disciples must count the cost before embarking on a commitment that they may find too difficult to complete (see Luke 14:28–33).

So there is a cost, a sacrifice involved in being a disciple of Jesus. But the gains far outweigh the cost. In Old Testament times 'sacrifice' meant the price of an animal to be offered on the altar. Now, God looks for a more fitting sacrifice, a sacrifice of love. Jesus commended an anonymous scribe who put it to him that love for God and love for neighbour were 'much more important than whole burnt offerings and sacrifices' (Mark 12:33). That is the 'sacrifice' that lies behind, and gives meaning to, all the other sacrifices of time, possessions and even relationships. They are the fruit of love, not of a cold, clinical demand by God. They are freely made, out of the overflow of a loving heart.

There is one other sacrifice in the Gospels which must be mentioned, and that is the sacrifice of Jesus himself. We shall be looking at this in more detail when we come to consider his death, but we should note here that Jesus does not ask more of his followers than he was prepared to give himself. His self-sacrifice—the offering of perfect obedience, on behalf of the disobedient—is the key to our forgiveness and the chief motive for our devotion to him. The Son of Man didn't come to make demands, but to offer himself for us. All our 'sacrifices' have to be seen in the light of that.

To REFLECT

David said, 'I will not offer burnt offerings to the Lord my God that cost me nothing' (2 Samuel 24:24). What is the 'cost' of my discipleship?

Other passages you may wish to consult: Mark 12:32–34; Luke 14:15–33; Luke 18:28–30

SATAN

MATTHEW 4:3−11

The tempter came and said to him, 'If you are the Son of God,
command these stones to become loaves of bread.' But he
answered, 'It is written, "One does not live by bread alone, but by
every word that comes from the mouth of God."' Then the devil
took him to the holy city and placed him on the pinnacle of the
temple, saying to him, 'If you are the Son of God, throw yourself
down; for it is written, "He will command his angels concerning
you," and "On their hands they will bear you up, so that you will
not dash your foot against a stone."' Jesus said to him, 'Again it is
written, "Do not put the Lord your God to the test."' Again, the
devil took him to a very high mountain and showed him all the
kingdoms of the world and their splendour; and he said to him, 'All
these I will give you, if you will fall down and worship me.' Jesus
said to him, 'Away with you, Satan! for it is written, "Worship the
Lord your God, and serve only him."' Then the devil left him, and
suddenly angels came and waited on him.

This well-known story of the temptation of Jesus encapsulates much
of his teaching about Satan, including three of the ways in which he
is described in the Gospels: the 'tempter' (v. 3), the 'devil' (v. 5) and
'Satan' (v. 10). He is also called 'Beelzebul' (Matthew 12:24) and 'the
ruler of this world' (John 14:30). There is nothing in the Gospels to
support the notion of a creature with horns and a forked tail—this is
the stuff of medieval horror stories—nor is Satan given the dignity of
human personality. The inference is that he is a being of angelic origin
and the focus of opposition to the will of God. Indeed, the name
'Satan' simply means 'adversary' or 'opponent'. We do not have to
subscribe to first-century ideas of demonology to recognize the reality
of that opposition, in the world, and in our own lives.

In this temptation narrative, found in very similar terms in Luke,
but only in brief summary in Mark, the nature of the conflict is set

out. Jesus, the 'Son of Man', has come to do God's will on earth and to proclaim his kingdom. This sets him on a collision course with the values and motives of Satan, personifying as he does all that is evil and negative in the world and in human nature. For Mark, most notably, the whole story of the mission of Jesus can be seen as a running battle between the powers of darkness, personified in Satan, and the power of God 'earthed' in his Son.

So Jesus in his 'temptation' was faced with several attractive alternatives to the costly and sacrificial course on which the Father had set him. He could use his miraculous powers for his own benefit (turning stones into bread). He could make an open show of his divinity, demanding belief by a single spectacular act—throwing himself down from a pinnacle of the temple. He could make worldly power and glory his goal, and by doing so put himself in Satan's hands. Each 'test' is confronted, considered and rejected, the devil's words countered by the words of scripture. The Son of God, at the outset of a mighty mission to confront and conquer evil, is himself tested to the utmost by its insidious attractions. This was a genuine 'test', fought out in the dusty arena of the human conscience of Jesus, an interior contest of the will that was costly and exhausting to win.

The battle was not over, of course. At every stage of the ministry of Jesus the 'enemy' reared his head, sometimes in human form (as this or that person took up the cause of the opposition), sometimes in the private area of the spirit (as in the Garden of Gethsemane—Matthew 26:39–42). It is the 'enemy' who plants weeds among the good seed (Matthew 13:25), it is the 'enemy' who snatches away that good seed when it falls on 'hard ground' (Matthew 13:19). Peter the apostle becomes himself 'the enemy', 'Satan', when he speaks in contradiction of the purpose of God (Matthew 16:23) and 'Satan' enters the heart of Judas when he sets out to betray Jesus (Luke 22:3). These instances should make us wary of too literal an interpretation of the person of Satan.

So the 'opposition' is fierce and awesome. Yet there could be only one victor in this battle. In one particularly sharp confrontation, in which Jesus faced both 'spiritual' evil and its human counterparts, he told those who had seen him cast out a demon: 'If it is by the finger of God that I cast out the demons, *then the kingdom of God has come to you'* (see Luke 11:14–20). The proof of the presence of the kingdom, in other words, was the defeat, by the power of God, of the powers of evil.

The seventy disciples had a similar experience when they returned to report on their mission. 'Lord', they said, 'in your name even the demons submit to us!' To which Jesus replied, 'I watched Satan fall from heaven like a flash of lightning… Nevertheless, do not rejoice at this, that the spirits submit to you, but rejoice that your names are written in heaven' (Luke 10:17–20).

This suggests that it is wrong to become obsessed with 'demons' and gaining victory over them. The real victory is discipleship, to have our names 'written in heaven'. And that victory belongs to the only one who could ever achieve it, the Son of God. The first letter of John puts it very succinctly: 'The Son of God was revealed for this purpose, to destroy the works of the devil' (1 John 3:8). It was through his obedience to God, through his total commitment to the will of the Father, through his divinely given authority, that Jesus could confront and defeat all that is evil in the world. This was his own private, lonely battle, finally won on the cross. All he calls us to do is to put our faith in what he has already done.

To REFLECT

A defeated enemy can still inflict wounds, but he cannot reverse the result of the war.

Other passages you may wish to consult: Matthew 12:43–45; Matthew 13:24–30; Matthew 16:21–23; Luke 22:3; Luke 22:31

SCRIPTURE

LUKE 24:25–32

> *Then (Jesus) said to them, 'Oh, how foolish you are, and how slow of heart to believe all that the prophets have declared! Was it not necessary that the Messiah should suffer these things and then enter into his glory?' Then beginning with Moses and all the prophets, he interpreted to them the things about himself in all the scriptures. As they came near the village to which they were going, he walked ahead as if he were going on. But they urged him strongly, saying, 'Stay with us, because it is almost evening and the day is now nearly over.' So he went in to stay with them. When he was at the table with them, he took bread, blessed and broke it, and gave it to them. Then their eyes were opened, and they recognized him; and he vanished from their sight. They said to each other, 'Were not our hearts burning within us while he was talking to us on the road, while he was opening the scriptures to us?'*

You can't get far into the teaching of Jesus without encountering the 'scriptures', especially in Matthew's Gospel. Sometimes the reference is slightly disguised by the use of some such phrase as 'It is written' or 'Have you not read?' but clearly he is referring to the 'holy writings'—the Law and the Prophets. The passage above, part of the story of the encounter of the risen Jesus with two of his disciples on the road to Emmaus, demonstrates how central to his teaching were the scriptures, here quite specifically described as 'Moses (that is, the Law) and the prophets'.

The word that Jesus used most frequently in connection with the scriptures was 'fulfilled': 'Let the scriptures be fulfilled' (Mark 14:49). Indeed, he seems to have seen his whole life and ministry as a fulfilment of the words of the prophets. If it had been foretold, then it must be 'fulfilled', even to his ignominious arrest, trial and execution (Matthew 26:54). There was no point in his friends fighting against this destiny: 'Let the scriptures be fulfilled'.

This could be regarded as a kind of fatalism, but that would be completely to misunderstand how Jesus saw both the prophetic scriptures and his own calling. He had not come on a 'solo mission'. He was not the origin or source of his own activity. He was *sent*, at the express bidding and will of the Father, to 'fulfil' a divine purpose for the salvation of the world. This purpose, while hidden from sceptical eyes, was there for all to see in 'the scriptures'—a truth he revealed to the doubting couple on their way home to Emmaus, heavy with the disappointment of his death and burial. It was to the scriptures that he turned their attention, rather than to his own resurrected presence with them. As devout Jews they should have known it: 'Was it not *necessary* that the Messiah should suffer these things and then enter into his glory?' And then, 'beginning with Moses and all the prophets', he gave them what must have been the most remarkable Bible study in history! No wonder that they recalled, after he had finally revealed himself to them 'in the breaking of the bread', that their hearts were 'burning within them' as they walked that long road and he 'opened the scriptures' to them (Luke 24:31, 32).

That raises the question of the human response to the scriptures. For Jesus, they not only had to be 'fulfilled', but they had to be 'opened', known and obeyed. Their blessings, in other words, are not automatic. When the Sadducees came with their trick question about the resurrection, Jesus told them that the reason they were wrong about it was that they knew 'neither the scriptures nor the power of God' (Mark 12:24). The two were comparable, for those who doubted the scriptures also doubted the power of God. In John's Gospel, Jesus is even more explicit, again in dispute with 'the Jews' (presumably the Jewish teachers). 'You search the scriptures', he said, 'because you think that in them you have eternal life; and it is they that testify on my behalf. Yet you refuse to come to me to have life' (John 5:39, 40). The power of the scriptures is the power of God, and it was that very power that was present in his Son. If they 'searched the scriptures' but failed to see it, then the scriptures themselves couldn't help them.

So Jesus didn't teach a kind of biblical fundamentalism. The God-given scriptures had to be read with faith and understanding—they were not magic. And Jesus himself showed on several occasions how a rigid attachment to the literal words (rather than their spiritual meaning) could actually distort the word of God. On one occasion, while Jesus and his disciples were walking through a field of grain on a sabbath day, his disciples plucked some heads of grain, rubbed them in their hands and ate them. The Pharisees claimed that in doing this on the sabbath they were acting unlawfully; and there's no doubt that they had the letter of the law on their side. But Jesus used the scriptures to demonstrate how David himself had broken the letter of the law in a moment of necessity, by eating the 'bread of the presence', which was strictly for the priests only. It was the principle that mattered, not the rigid enforcement of a text (see Luke 6:1–5).

The 'scriptures' that Jesus knew, and that sustained him even in his hours of agony, were what we would call the Old Testament. He would have heard them from his earliest infant years, recited them in the synagogue, learnt them by heart. For him, the will of God, which he had come to fulfil, and the scriptures, which 'must be fulfilled', were one and the same thing. Properly understood, they were the key to truth.

To REFLECT

'I will delight in your statutes; I will not forget your word' (Psalm 119:16). *For Jesus, the scriptures were not a burden, but a joy.*

SIN

MATTHEW 15:11, 17–20

It is not what goes into the mouth that defiles a person, but it is what comes out of the mouth that defiles.' ... Do you not see that whatever goes into the mouth enters the stomach, and goes out into the sewer? But what comes out of the mouth proceeds from the heart, and this is what defiles. For out of the heart come evil intentions, murder, adultery, fornication, theft, false witness, slander. These are what defile a person, but to eat with unwashed hands does not defile.'

While it would be an exaggeration to say that Jesus was always 'going on about sin', it would be true to say that he had an acute eye for its presence in individuals, and in society. Indeed, his denunciation of 'sins', which was on occasions very fierce, was only matched by his generous welcome to 'sinners', which earned him the nickname from the scribes, 'the friend of sinners'. But the very use of the single word 'sin' disguises the fact that the English word is used to translate several quite different Greek words, and quite different ideas.

Often Jesus used a word which is the basis of our word 'scandal' (so, for example, 'sin' in Matthew 5:29–30, or in Mark 9:42). A 'scandal' in this sense is a cause of offence, something over which other people stumble. But the word came also to mean the offence or sin itself—something that offended or shocked, something repugnant. It speaks of the ugliness of 'sin'. But it also speaks of sin as personal failure, 'stumbling', or as we might say, 'falling'. Much of what is normally associated with 'sin' in ordinary usage is covered by this word.

At other times a Greek word is used which means 'fault' or 'flaw'. This is most commonly used when sin is to be seen in the light of God's judgment. So 'whoever blasphemes against the Holy Spirit can never have forgiveness, but is guilty of an eternal sin' (Mark 3:29). This word literally means 'falling short' or 'missing the mark', and is a vivid description of what sin is in the eyes of a holy God. We 'fall short'. We 'miss the mark'. The goal of moral perfection is set before us, but we simply cannot attain it. So this particular word speaks of a failure to meet God's exacting standards: sin is our 'fault'.

But its meaning also includes the idea of sin as a 'flaw', and that is perhaps nearer to the way that Jesus usually speaks of it in human experience. Sin is the tragic flaw that spoils life, destroys our peace of mind, robs us of purpose and direction and, most seriously of all, cuts us off from God. That idea lies behind the word which Jesus frequently uses to describe 'sinners'—the 'lost'. It is a much less ugly and forbidding term than 'sinner', and places the flawed human being in a position that we can readily understand. He or she is still valuable in the sight of God, still the object of Christ's loving concern, but has drifted away from the fixed points and moral references that can give shape and meaning to life. There's a particularly touching example of this when Jesus, seeing the crowds, 'had compassion for them, because they were harassed and helpless, like sheep without a shepherd' (Matthew 9:36). He had come, he said, to 'seek out and to save the lost' (Luke 19:10).

In the passage set out at the head of this chapter the actual word 'sin' does not occur, but there is an ugly list of human failings, all of which could generally be put under that heading: 'evil intentions, murder, adultery, fornication, theft, false witness, slander'. These are things that 'defile' a person, says Jesus. They are causes of stumbling and they are serious and destructive flaws and moral failures. The point he is making, of course, is that these are not primarily the product of outside influences, but of inner intention: sin is a matter of personal, moral responsibility, a responsibility that can't be transferred to others, or to circumstances.

I think it would be going too far to say that Jesus discounted other factors, such as nurture, environment and peer pressure: his gentle treatment of the woman taken in adultery (John 8:11) or of the woman 'who was a sinner' who gatecrashed the Pharisee's dinner party (Luke 7:47) suggests that he knew life is not lived on a level playing-field for everyone. But his argument here is powerful: we cannot escape responsibility for our own actions. Evil comes from the heart of fallen humanity, and therefore the heart must be changed if the behaviour is to be changed. The Pharisees' obsession with outward washings was futile. It was the inner person that needed to be cleansed.

This is consistent with the teaching of Jesus about good and evil deeds. Good deeds emanate from a good heart, and evil deeds emanate from an evil one. That may sound obvious, but in fact it is a profound analysis of cause and effect. Those who have stored the 'good treasure' of the kingdom in their hearts will naturally produce good things. Those who have stored in their hearts the evil of greed or malice will inevitably bring forth evil things. So 'make the tree good, and its fruit good' (Matthew 12:33)—a recurrent note in the teaching of Jesus. It is all a question of tackling root causes rather than symptoms.

But the really distinctive thing about Jesus' teaching on sin is his love for the sinner. One cannot read the Gospels without being struck by his concern to rescue the lost, seek out the failures, lift up the fallen and bring forgiveness and new life to those who turn to him. Yes, he saw sin as an offence against God and a blasphemous distortion of his creation. But his harshest words were reserved for those who preferred to cover up sin or deny its presence. For the one whose destiny was to be the Saviour of the world, his earthly life was a demonstration in microcosm of that eternal purpose. On the cross he would die for the 'sins of the world', but in the dusty lanes of Galilee he sought out and saved one sinner and another who turned to him. He was, one could say, 'that sort of person'.

To REFLECT

'This fellow welcomes sinners and eats with them' (Luke 15:2).
And yet 'this fellow' denounced sin with a ferocity that those who heard his words could never forget. That paradox is at the heart of the mystery of the Son of God on earth.

Other passages you may wish to consult: Matthew 13:24–30, 37–43; Matthew 23:25–26; Matthew 26:27, 28; Mark 7:18–23

DAY 34 (SATURDAY)

SUFFERING

LUKE 13:1-3

At that very time there were some present who told him about the Galileans whose blood Pilate had mingled with their sacrifices. He asked them, 'Do you think that because these Galileans suffered in this way they were worse sinners than all other Galileans? No, I tell you; but unless you repent, you will all perish as they did.'

MATTHEW 11:28-30

'Come to me, all you that are weary and are carrying heavy burdens, and I will give you rest. Take my yoke upon you, and learn from me; for I am gentle and humble in heart, and you will find rest for your souls. For my yoke is easy, and my burden is light.'

The problem of suffering has exercised Christians all through the history of the Church. How can a good and loving God allow his creatures to suffer as they do? Why, in a good creation, is there cancer, earthquake, flood and plague? Why do innocent children suffer? There can't be many of us who haven't at some time asked these questions.

Although the time of Christ was a time of enormous suffering, both from natural and human causes, the Jewish mind did not agonize as we do over the divine responsibility for suffering. It is a relatively modern idea to hold God 'guilty', as it were, for the pain and anguish of the world. In Jewish thought, all that happened was the will of God. The evil were penalized and the good prospered. So it was a simple deduction to assume that if you suffered—from poverty, illness or accident—it was in some way your fault, and what had happened to you was a kind of divine judgment. This was the awful premise that made the suffering of Job so appalling. On the other hand, if you prospered—your crops increased, your family flourished—then it was a sign of God's approval.

On the occasion described above, some bystanders made this

point to Jesus. Some Galileans had been massacred, apparently as they were making their sacrifices to God. Did this prove, as was commonly believed, that they were 'worse sinners' than everybody else in the country? The answer of Jesus is categorical, reinforced by his typical 'I tell you': No, certainly not. But, he added, *all* should practise repentance, or judgment would fall on all. In Luke's account Jesus then added a further instance, of some people who were killed by a collapsing tower in Siloam, in Jerusalem. Were they, he asked the crowd, 'worse offenders' than everybody else in the city? Again, 'I tell you'—No. They were the victims of an *accident*, no more, and no less. Suffering is *not* punishment by God, any more than success is a sign of his approval. After all, as the psalmist pointed out, 'the evil flourish like the bay tree' (Psalm 37:35, *Book of Common Prayer*)!

The same point is made in a story in John's Gospel, where Jesus is confronted by a man who was born blind. His disciples, employing the assumptions that they had been taught from childhood, asked whether this was the result of his own sin, or his parents'—it *must* be a consequence of someone's moral failure. Again the answer of Jesus is categorical: 'neither this man nor his parents sinned' (John 9:2, 3). So we can be absolutely clear from the teaching of Jesus that human suffering is not the result of individual human sin, in a direct cause and effect way. Of course, human sin in a *collective* way may have a great deal to do with human suffering, in terms of poverty, hunger, homelessness, injustice, violence and so on. But individuals who suffer are not being punished by God. When a bereaved person asks, understandably, 'Why should this happen to him? He never did anyone any harm', they are expressing an intensely human reaction to the random nature of suffering. But the correct Christian response is to assure them that whatever the cause of that suffering, it is not willed by God, nor is it his punishment for anyone's sin.

The other passage quoted above, the well-loved 'words of comfort' of Jesus, serves as a balance to the widespread idea that God is remote from the day-to-day suffering of his creatures. For those who 'come' to him, Jesus offers rest and relief from the burden. Indeed, and more than that, he offers to share it, as an oxen shares the load with its partner under the yoke. So, 'you will find rest for your souls'. This is the key to understanding a truly Christian response to suffering.

During the Falklands War an Argentinian warship, the *Belgrano*, was sunk by a British missile, with the loss of its entire crew. My colleague at the BBC at the time, Colin Semper, was the speaker on 'Thought for the Day' that morning. He said that someone had asked him sceptically, 'Where was your God when the *Belgrano* went down?' Colin's reply was short, memorable, and utterly consistent with the teaching of Jesus: 'He was in the boat with them.' God is not detached from human suffering, but totally involved in it. The whole life and ministry of Jesus makes that point—and so, of course, even more powerfully, does his death. The cross is the final proof of God's intimate involvement in the suffering of his creatures.

To REFLECT

> The invitation of Jesus is to those who are 'weary and carrying heavy burdens'. The offer is to share the load and make the burden 'light'.

Other passages you may wish to consult: Matthew 5:4, 10, 11; Matthew 26:38–42; Mark 8:31–37; Mark 13:19, 20; Luke 12:6, 7

HOLY WEEK

PAUSE *for* PRAYER

MATTHEW 21:9

*The crowds that went ahead of him and that followed were
shouting, 'Hosanna to the Son of David! Blessed is the one who
comes in the name of the Lord! Hosanna in the highest heaven!'*

Today the cry goes up, 'Hosanna!' By next Friday, though almost
certainly from different lips, it has become 'Crucify him!' Human
beings are dangerously susceptible to their feelings—doubly so when
they are in a crowd. The crowds play a major role in the story of Holy
Week.

But let us pause to consider the word 'hosanna', which is frequently used in Christian worship, not only on Palm Sunday. It's one
of the few Hebrew words that have survived the rendering of the
Gospel stories into Greek. Literally it simply means 'Save!' but it
came to be used as an expression of adoration and praise. The one
who can 'save' us is obviously far greater than we are. Our 'saviour'
is the one who comes to our aid, rescues us, gets us out of trouble.
So the crowd—probably of Galilean disciples—shouted 'Hosanna!'
at Jesus. 'Be our Saviour! Rescue us! Deliver us from the hands of our
enemies! You are like the great king David. You come to us in the
name of the Lord. Bring us salvation from heaven above!'

They had both got it right and got it wrong, of course. But what
they had not got wrong was the very heart of Christian worship: a
whole-hearted sense of dependence, of adoration, of gratitude to the
one who has saved us. With or without a palm branch, we can join
them in that.

A PRAYER

Saviour, King, accept my worship. You are worthy!

WORSHIP

MATTHEW 26:6–13

Now while Jesus was at Bethany in the house of Simon the leper, a woman came to him with an alabaster jar of very costly ointment, and she poured it on his head as he sat at the table. But when the disciples saw it, they were angry and said, 'Why this waste? For this ointment could have been sold for a large sum, and the money given to the poor.' But Jesus, aware of this, said to them, 'Why do you trouble the woman? She has performed a good service for me. For you always have the poor with you, but you will not always have me. By pouring this ointment on my body she has prepared me for burial. Truly I tell you, wherever this good news is proclaimed in the whole world, what she has done will be told in remembrance of her.'

It is easier to find occasions in the teaching of Jesus where he was scathing about the hypocrisy of much that passed for 'worship' among his contemporaries than it is to find positive guidance on true worship. Clearly he was distressed by the abuse of the temple (see, for instance, Mark 11:15–17—the 'cleansing of the temple') and appalled at outward shows of piety not matched by inward devotion. The Pharisees prayed 'at the street corners, so that they might be seen by others' (Matthew 6:5). Well, 'they have received their reward', in public approval. For Jesus, it was God's approval that mattered: 'Your Father who sees in secret will reward you' (Matthew 6:6). Yet he was regularly and publicly in the synagogue on the sabbath day (Luke 4:16) and his anger at the desecration of the temple was not because he did not value the institution, but because 'zeal for your house will consume me' (John 2:17). A good thing was being misused.

Jesus set his own clear priorities where worship of God was concerned. He commended a scribe who argued that to love God with heart, understanding and strength, and 'one's neighbour as oneself' was 'more important than all whole burnt offerings and sacrifices' (Mark 12:33). This seems to have been his own understanding of true worship—a recognition of the uniqueness of God and his call on our love and obedience, and a reverence and love for all those made in his image, our 'neighbours'. So, while outward rituals and prayers could play an important part in this, they were only *means* to worship, not the thing itself. True worship was, quite simply, putting God first, others second, and oneself last. The sin of the Pharisees was to use worship as a means of self-promotion, rather than as a means to glorify God.

But there is another element to worship, which goes far beyond the question of form or even content, and that is love for God. It is hinted at in the words of the good scribe ('to love God… is more important than burnt offerings'), but demonstrated most vividly in the lovely story set out at the head of this chapter, of the anointing of Jesus at Bethany, just before his arrest and crucifixion. While he was at dinner in the house of Simon 'the leper', a woman came with an alabaster jar of 'very costly' ointment, and poured it on his head as he sat at table. Some of the disciples protested at this apparently wasteful gesture, pointing out that the ointment could have been sold for a 'large sum' and 'the money given to the poor'. They probably expected Jesus, who was always very concerned about the needs of the poor, to agree with them.

But he didn't. On the contrary, he rebuked them. 'Why do you trouble the woman? She has performed a good service for me.' Indeed, he said, she has 'prepared me for burial'—anointed me, as it were. 'Truly I tell you, wherever this good news is proclaimed in the whole world, what she has done will be told in remembrance of her.'

For Jesus, this was a true act of 'worship', arising from a deep devotion and love, perhaps based on gratitude for healing or forgiveness. Such an act of worship is spontaneous, generous and sacrificial—in fact, it borders on the irrational. The woman's action was simply the outpouring of an inner well of love, like a spring bursting out of a hillside. Normal criteria of propriety or restraint could not be applied to it. This was how she felt, and this was how she expressed it.

The whole story echoes, in an individual's actions, the principle which is expressed in the Gospel of John, in the strange dialogue between Jesus and the Samaritan woman at the well. At the end of a conversation which skirted around the differences between the Jewish and Samaritan practices of worship, Jesus brought the discussion to a conclusion with these words: 'The hour is coming, and is now here, when the true worshippers will worship the Father in spirit and in truth, for the Father seeks such as these to worship him. God is spirit, and those who worship him must worship in spirit and in truth' (John 4:23, 24).

The language is that of the fourth Gospel, but the principle is very close to that praised by Jesus at the home of Simon. True worship is not calculated, cool, methodical. It flows from a true heart, motivated by a spirit of love and gratitude, and wells up in costly, generous and spontaneous devotion. While the Pharisees dotted the liturgical 'i's and crossed the ceremonial 't's, this woman had found the secret of true worship. In temple, synagogue, church or home, it is the heart that worships, and without the worship of the heart, words are empty and ritual meaningless.

To REFLECT

The well-spring of worship is a 'glad and generous heart' (Acts 2:46). How can my outward praise express that inward devotion?

Other passages you may wish to consult: Matthew 14:28–33; Mark 7:1–8

Day 36 (Tuesday)

Jesus' teaching about Himself:
His Identity

MARK 8:27–32

> Jesus went on with his disciples to the villages of Caesarea Philippi;
> and on the way he asked his disciples, 'Who do people say that I
> am?' And they answered him, 'John the Baptist; and others,
> Elijah; and still others, one of the prophets.' He asked them, 'But
> who do you say that I am?' Peter answered him, 'You are the
> Messiah.' And he sternly ordered them not to tell anyone about
> him. Then he began to teach them that the Son of Man must
> undergo great suffering, and be rejected by the elders, the chief
> priests, and the scribes, and be killed, and after three days rise
> again. He said all this quite openly.

Here is the question that haunts every reader of the Gospels: who *is*
he? Of course, he is 'Jesus of Nazareth', the son of the carpenter and
Mary. It is also obvious that Jesus was a magnetic and charismatic
figure, a preacher and teacher who inspired devotion among his
followers and attracted huge crowds to hear him. And both the
Gospels and secular history record his formidable reputation as a
healer. But most people reading the Gospels have felt that there was
more to this person even than that.

The same problem faced his disciples, and it came to a head in this
intriguing moment in the north of Galilee, at Caesarea Philippi. As
they were walking, Jesus asked them who people thought he was.
They were ready with several replies to that: John the Baptist, Elijah,
'one of the prophets'. But then came the question that they could
avoid no longer, and one that they had presumably been talking over
among themselves: 'Who do *you* say that I am?' When Peter spoke,
we may assume that he spoke for them all: 'You are the Messiah.'

They would later come to the conclusion—after the resurrection
and Pentecost, perhaps—that Jesus was more than that: Saviour of
the world, Son of God, even that he bore the divine nature in human

form. But at this stage it was sufficient that they could make this enormous leap of faith—and it *was* enormous for a group of devout and orthodox Jews. If Jesus was truly the Messiah of God, then the man with whom they shared their days and nights was none other than the promised and anointed Saviour of Israel. We may assume that they did not come to such a conclusion lightly.

This dialogue is typical of the way in which Jesus tended to treat the subject of his 'identity'. He made few claims for himself. Indeed, in the synoptic Gospels there is no explicit claim made by Jesus that he was the Messiah, much less the 'Son of God'. As we shall see, his own preferred self-title was 'Son of Man', which is quite a different thing. But while he never explicitly claimed messiahship (in so many words), he accepted the title from others, and indeed said that the confession made by Peter ('You are the Messiah') was a matter of divine revelation: 'Flesh and blood has not revealed this to you, but my Father in heaven' (Matthew 16:17). He also, in very solemn circumstances, answered the high priest's question, 'Are you the Messiah, the Son of the Blessed One?' with a clear affirmative: 'I am' (Mark 14:61, 62).

However, the disclosure of his messiahship is often treated—especially in Mark's Gospel—as a 'secret', only to be revealed to faith. Far from crying this great truth from the roof-tops, Jesus time and again urged people (or even 'demons') who had 'discovered' it not to tell anyone (see, for instance, Mark 1:43, 44; 3:11, 12; 5:43; 7:36; 8:29, 30). The 'secret' of his true identity was only for those who had put their faith in him. 'To you [that is, the disciples] has been given the secret of the kingdom of God, but for those outside, everything comes in parables' (Mark 4:11, 12).

This seems to have been partly because Jesus saw his role in terms of the fulfilment of the scriptures, and he wished the people to see him as the long-promised Saviour of Israel now come to them, exactly as the prophets had said he would. As he once told his disciples, 'Everything that is written about the Son of Man by the prophets will be accomplished' (Luke 18:31). His life was not an accident and his calling was clear to him, even if hidden from others.

So that leaves the important question: who did *Jesus* think he was? There seems no doubt at all that he knew himself to be the Messiah, the 'one who is to come' that John the Baptist enquired about. The answer of Jesus to the disciples sent by John to find out whether he was indeed that 'one' was to offer the evidence of his deeds: 'The blind receive their sight, the lame walk, the lepers are cleansed, the deaf hear, the dead are raised and the poor have good news brought to them' (Matthew 11:2–6). These are precisely the promised blessings of the coming Messiah (Isaiah 61:1, 2). The evidence was the fulfilment of the prophecy. Who, looking at the evidence, could doubt that the Lord's anointed (the literal meaning of *messiah*) was among them?

As we shall see, he was not to be quite the kind of Messiah the people of his time expected. His model was less the kingly conqueror in the mould of David, more the 'suffering servant' of the Lord foretold by Isaiah (see Isaiah 53). But that he *was* that anointed one, who had come to save his people, seems to have been the central truth of his whole ministry.

To REFLECT

The Messiah was to be a man, like Adam; a saviour, like Moses; and a king, like David. It's worth reflecting on those three images in seeking to establish the true 'identity' of Jesus—Son of Man, Saviour, and Lord.

Other passages you may wish to consult: Matthew 11:2–6; Luke 18:31–33

DAY 37 (WEDNESDAY)

Jesus' teaching about Himself:
SON of MAN

LUKE 19:10

'For the Son of Man came to seek out and to save the lost.'

LUKE 6:5

Then he said to them, 'The Son of Man is lord of the sabbath.'

MATTHEW 16:27

'For the Son of Man is to come with his angels in the glory of his Father, and then he will repay everyone for what has been done.'

Whole books, and many of them, have been written about the precise meaning of the title 'Son of Man', or even whether it is a title at all. However, this book is about what Jesus said, rather than what others have said about him, and we shall confine ourselves as far as we can to what he said, and the way in which he seemed to interpret the words.

There can be no doubt of one thing. This was how Jesus customarily referred to himself: 'Who do people say that *the Son of Man* is?' (Matthew 16:13), followed by 'But who do you say that *I* am?' (v. 15). Clearly, for Jesus 'the Son of Man' and 'I' were the same person. Although the phrase is a common enough one in its Hebrew or Aramaic form, and could mean little more than 'human', there seems no doubt that Jesus was investing it with a particular significance and meaning. Indeed, his addition of the definite article 'the' before it suggests that he is talking about a particular 'son of man'.

If we ask which particular one, the most likely answer must be the 'son of man' mentioned in the prophecy of Daniel (see Daniel 10:18—'one who looked like a man', NIV; 'one in human form', NRSV). This being is addressed by the prophet as 'Lord' and is imbued with divine power and authority. Although speaking with the authority of God and acting at the very least as his emissary, he is nevertheless human. He is 'a son of man', rather than an angel. So the phrase entered the religion of Israel, surfacing from time to time in the post-exilic period and in the Dead Sea scrolls, though seldom defined beyond the notion of a human being with special power to act for God.

But now, with Jesus, we have not *a* son of man but *the* Son of Man: a human being who is 'lord of the sabbath'—surely only God himself can claim that? A human being who will one day sit in judgment on the world—surely only God himself could do that? Here is a unique title for a unique person, a title that incorporates many ideas from the Hebrew scriptures and from the religious thought of the time, but invests itself with an entirely new insight into the nature and purposes of God.

Jesus is the Son of Man. That is to say, he is fully and completely human. There were those in the early days of the Church who found that a difficult truth to accept. The Gnostics believed that matter itself was sinful, so how could God 'enflesh' himself in what was sinful? They wanted a Jesus who was a spirit-visitor from another world (and sometimes that's an error that creeps into Christian preaching and devotion today). But he wasn't. Jesus was completely, robustly, absolutely human, 'born of a woman', in the apostle Paul's phrase. It is as a human being that he can stand with us, be 'for' us, and even, in the mystery of salvation, stand 'in place of' us. As the first letter to Timothy puts it, 'There is one God; there is also one mediator between God and humankind, Christ Jesus, *himself human*' (2:5). It is no exaggeration to say that if Jesus was not fully and truly human then he could not be the Saviour of human beings.

Then, as the Son of Man, he also stood under the authority of his Father. This is a persistent element in the teaching of Jesus, especially —but not exclusively—in the fourth Gospel. We have seen already how Jesus uses the phrase, 'The Son of Man *must*...' That 'must' is the will of the Father, often revealed through the scriptures. Jesus on earth was a 'man under authority' (see Luke 7:8), but that authority was his Father's, not an earthly power or man-made regulation.

The third element of the meaning of this title is the most elusive one. While the Son of Man was emphatically human and operated on earth under the authority of his Father, yet he himself shared the divine nature. He was not only Son of Man but Son of God. The way in which Jesus answered the high priest at his trial is very revealing. The high priest said to him, 'I put you under oath before the living God, tell us if you are the Messiah, the Son of God'. Jesus answered, 'You have said so. But I tell you, From now on you will see the *Son of Man* seated at the right hand of Power and coming on the clouds of heaven' (Matthew 26:63, 64). A modern reader might see that as a rather ambiguous answer; was he the Son of God, or not? Yet the high priest apparently had no doubt as to its meaning, tearing his clothes and screaming, 'He has blasphemed!' (v. 65).

The 'Power' is, of course, God himself. The seat at his right hand is for his Son, and it is a place of divine authority. At the end of Matthew's Gospel Jesus tells his still doubtful disciples, 'All authority in heaven and on earth has been given to me' (28:18). That is some claim for a 'mere' mortal! But the Son of Man, one of us, is also the Son of God, 'seated at the right hand of Power'. That is both awesome and wonderfully comforting.

To REFLECT

'The Son of Man goes as it is written of him' (Matthew 26:24):
goes, of course, to the cross. This 'Son of Man' identified so
completely with us that he even shared our final hurdle,
death itself.

Other passages you may wish to consult: Matthew 17:9–12; Luke 19:10; 1 John 4:2

DAY 38 (MAUNDY THURSDAY)

Jesus' teaching about Himself:
SON of GOD

MATTHEW 11:25–30

At that time Jesus said, 'I thank you, Father, Lord of heaven and earth, because you have hidden these things from the wise and the intelligent and have revealed them to infants; yes, Father, for such was your gracious will. All things have been handed over to me by my Father; and no one knows the Son except the Father, and no one knows the Father except the Son and anyone to whom the Son chooses to reveal him. Come to me, all you that are weary and are carrying heavy burdens, and I will give you rest. Take my yoke upon you, and learn from me; for I am gentle and humble in heart, and you will find rest for your souls. For my yoke is easy and my burden is light.'

Messiah, Son of Man—do these titles exhaust the answers to the question, 'Who is Jesus?' The Gospel writers would want to say, 'No, they don't', because by the time they were compiling their 'biographies' of Jesus, the Church had come to the unshakeable conviction that he was also, and supremely, the Son of God. Over the centuries this belief became the bedrock of the Christian faith. Those who believed it were Christians. Those who did not were heretics, of one kind or another. The 'nature' of Jesus was the touchstone of orthodoxy: he was, as the Nicene Creed says, 'of one Being with the Father... God from God... true God from true God'. There can be no doubt that this is the teaching of the Church.

But was it part of the teaching of Jesus himself? Or is this, as some have claimed, an honour the Church bestowed which he would have found embarrassing and even blasphemous? He seems to have claimed messiahship in a quite unambiguous way, and his own chosen title, 'Son of Man', certainly speaks of a unique role in the working of God. But did he actually claim divinity? Did he see *himself* as the Son of God in a way that is different from that experienced by other 'children of the Father'?

To try to answer that, we might look first at his words and then at his actions. All the while, we must recognize a principle that we saw when considering his messiahship—that he wanted people to come to their understanding of his nature and role through *faith*, through receiving God's revelation rather than recognizing visible proofs. So in this realm, too, his words are sometimes deliberately tentative, even obscure. We could cite his answer, as Luke gives it, to the Council's question, 'Are you, then, the Son of God?' Jesus replied, 'You say that I am' (Luke 22:70). The words in Greek are deceptively simple— literally as that version gives them. Yet, not without justification, the NIV translates them, 'You are right in saying that I am'—an interpretation supported by the response of the Council members: 'What further testimony do we need? We have heard it ourselves from his own lips!'

Mark's version of the reply of Jesus to a similar question from the high priest is much less ambiguous. 'Are you... the Son of the Blessed One?' he was asked, to which his reply was simply, 'I am' (Mark 14:62). When a man possessed by demons identified him as 'Jesus, Son of the Most High God', there was no attempt to deny it or to contradict this identification (Luke 8:28). So we can say that while Jesus nowhere in the synoptic Gospels directly set out to assert his divinity (his 'shared nature' with God), he also did not deny it. That is clearly very significant. His response to the confession of Peter—'You are the Messiah, the Son of the living God'—was not to deny it, but to assure him that this had been revealed to Peter not by 'flesh and blood' (human reason) but by 'my Father in heaven' (Matthew 16:16).

The passage set out at the head of this chapter is probably the clearest statement about his nature in the synoptic Gospels. It is a clear claim that 'the Father' has revealed to those who have childlike faith the great truth that Jesus is the unique revelation of God. That seems to be the only possible interpretation of verse 27. It is because of that 'special relationship' between Father and Son that Jesus can call people to come to himself: 'Come to *me*, all you that are weary...' It is hard to believe that any sane person would have made such claims about himself unless he believed them to be true, fantastic as they sound.

When we turn to consider what Jesus *did*, we find a consistent pattern, which would reveal to the eye of faith his special identity. He forgave sins, not as the scribes did, by invoking the forgiveness of God, but in his own name and on his own authority (see Mark 2:7). He took it upon himself to act as a reinterpreter (in a fairly fundamental way!) of the Law of God. For example, see Matthew 5:33–34, 38–39 and so on: 'You have heard that it was said to those of ancient times...' (he was referring, of course, to the Law of Moses, no less!) He then went on: 'But *I* say to you...' That was either a bogus and blasphemous claim to divine authority, or a demonstration that he possessed it. No other conclusion seems possible.

Then there was the way Jesus addressed God as *Abba*, one of the few Aramaic words which are preserved in the Gospel texts (see Mark 14:36). This seems to have been a distinctive feature of his teaching about God. At any rate, no one has yet been able to find a clear case of anyone before Jesus using this intimate and homely form of address for the deity. Instead of the dignified *pater* he substituted the much more familiar *abba*, the name children would have used as they climbed on daddy's knee. It was an indication of his own intimacy with the Father, as well as an invitation to his followers to share in that new relationship of dependent love.

On one occasion Jesus referred to an exorcism that he had carried out as being accomplished 'by the finger of God' (Luke 11:20). This is an intriguing phrase, full of Old Testament overtones (see, for instance, Exodus 8:19). After all, it was the very finger of God that inscribed the Commandments on the tablets of stone (Exodus 31:18). This phrase speaks of God's own personal involvement, acting not through an intermediary but directly. Yet that is exactly the way in which Jesus described his own action in casting out the evil spirits. It is, at the very least, a claim that in his actions God was not acting through an intermediary but directly and personally.

But the most telling evidence for the divine Sonship of Jesus is the totality of his life. I do not believe that anyone reading and reflecting on the life of Jesus as the Gospels present it would doubt that Jesus represented the incarnation of God, God 'with a human face'. As John's Gospel puts it, 'Whoever has seen me has seen the Father' (John 14:9). That is the overwhelming testimony of the records, one to which the centurion at the crucifixion made his own moving contribution. 'Truly,' he exclaimed, 'this man was God's Son!' He wouldn't have meant by that remark all that a Christian would wish to invest in it, but it was a solemn testimonial by an impartial witness to the way this man died—and nothing, they say, tells you more about the character of a person that that.

Some years ago we had a young friend, an actor and singer, who was cast as Jesus in *Jesus Christ Superstar* in London's West End. When he got the part he rang me up and asked if I could give him some 'background reading'—he admitted to knowing next to nothing about Jesus. I lent him the four Gospels, in J.B. Phillips' translation. He phoned me in high excitement the next day, having devoured them more or less at a sitting. 'It seems to me,' he said, 'that if this guy wasn't the Son of God, then his scriptwriter was.'

To REFLECT

What difference does it make to the way I think about and respond to the teaching of Jesus if I recognize him as the Son of God?

Other passages you may wish to consult: Matthew 22:41–45; Matthew 28:18–20; Luke 10:22; Luke 11:31, 32

DAY 39 (GOOD FRIDAY)

Jesus' teaching about Himself:
HIS DEATH

MARK 10:45

> 'For the Son of Man came not to be served but to serve,
> and to give his life a ransom for many.'

MATTHEW 20:17–19

> While Jesus was going up to Jerusalem, he took the twelve disciples
> aside by themselves, and said to them on the way, 'See, we are
> going up to Jerusalem, and the Son of Man will be handed over to
> the chief priests and scribes, and they will condemn him to death;
> then they will hand him over to the Gentiles to be mocked and
> flogged and crucified; and on the third day he will be raised.'

Nobody could possibly describe Jesus as morbid, yet it's a fact that a
recurring theme of his teaching, especially from the time of the transfiguration onwards, was his own death. He seems to have seen it as
the fulfilment of his destiny, part of the divine purpose at work in his
life, rather than a personal tragedy. 'The Son of man *must* suffer...'
(Mark 8:31, NIV).

This ran counter to the popular view of what the coming of the
Messiah would mean, but it was very much in line with the image of
the 'suffering servant of the Lord' depicted by Isaiah: 'He (the "Lord's
servant") was despised and rejected by others; a man of suffering and
acquainted with infirmity... He was cut off from the land of the
living, stricken for the transgression of my people' (53:3, 8).
Although the public mind rejected this image of the Messiah, such
ideas were current in Jewish thought in the first century. We know
this from the Dead Sea scrolls, which sometimes take a far from
triumphalist view of the role of the Messiah.

But Jesus' teaching on his destiny was on a different plane entirely.
There is no anger or bitterness in his words. This is how it will be,
solely and uniquely because this is how the Father has willed it. His

death would not be simply a stunning act of human injustice, but the fulfilment of God's great purpose of salvation. He had come to be their servant, and to 'give his life a ransom for many'. His death, as he said at his last supper with his disciples, would be 'for the forgiveness of sins' (Matthew 26:28). Far from being a meaningless act of violence or injustice, carried out by mean-minded religious bigots, it would be the magnificent culmination and fulfilment of everything he had taught and everything the Father had willed. When Peter rebelled against the very idea of Jesus suffering at the hands of the elders and chief priests, he was speaking with the voice of Satan, acting as a 'stumbling block' to the fulfilment of the divine purpose (Matthew 16:23). The journey to the cross was not to be seen by them as a disaster: 'The Son of Man is going as it has been determined' (Luke 22:22).

The use by Jesus of the word 'ransom' is very significant. It seems to point inescapably to that same passage in Isaiah, where the Lord's servant 'bore the sin of many' (53:12). A 'ransom' is, of course, the price paid for liberty, and Jesus had already applied other words of Isaiah to himself: 'He has sent me to proclaim release to the captives' (Luke 4:18, compare Isaiah 61:1). A central part of the work of Jesus as Saviour was to release people from the 'captivity' of sin, and if that involved a 'price', he was prepared to pay it. In fact, the 'price' was his own life, paid as a 'ransom for many'—an exact echo of Isaiah 53:12. It is fruitless to ask to whom the price was to be paid. That is not, either here or in Isaiah, the central question. What is at stake is the freedom of people made in God's image, but now in captivity to sin and death. The 'price' of their freedom is high, because sin itself is not some minor blemish but a major defilement of the creation. Indeed, the price is so high that only the death of the Son of God can achieve it—not as an enforced demand, one should note, but as a gift of grace: 'to *give* his life a ransom for many'.

Much of this teaching about the death of Jesus is made more explicit in the Gospel of John. He would be 'lifted up' on the cross and draw 'all people' to himself (John 12:32). The 'grain of wheat' must die and fall into the ground in order to bear 'much fruit' (John 12:24). 'As Moses lifted up the serpent in the wilderness, so must the Son of Man be lifted up, that whoever believes in him may have eternal life' (John 3:14, 15). But the synoptic Gospels are equally clear. Indeed, in one sense they are more explicit about the death of

Jesus as the fulfilment of God's purpose. All that Jesus is, and all that he taught, was to be made effective by two great events, his death and his resurrection. 'See, we are going up to Jerusalem, and the Son of Man will be handed over... to be mocked and flogged and crucified; and on the third day he will be raised' (Matthew 20:18–19). Even those who presume that the explicit references to the resurrection are not part of the actual words of Jesus at that time must accept that this teaching is right at the heart of the synoptic tradition. It was an essential part of the teaching about Jesus handed on through the apostles.

And that is consistent with the whole picture of his ministry. Without the cross, and all it means for forgiveness of sins, much of the moral teaching of Jesus is unrealistic, way beyond human achieving. And without the resurrection we have no guarantee that Jesus was not just another splendid but failed prophet, no more than a sad footnote in the history of the human race. His death and resurrection, when seen as part of the whole saving purpose of God, put everything else into perspective. He was all that he claimed to be. He achieved all that he had been sent to do. This is indeed the Saviour of the world.

To REFLECT

Probably the greatest single act of injustice in human history—the execution of Jesus—is also, in God's purpose, the greatest single act of love the world has ever seen.

DAY 40 (HOLY SATURDAY)

Jesus' teaching about Himself:
HIS PURPOSE

LUKE 4:16–21

*When he came to Nazareth, where he had been brought up, he
went to the synagogue on the sabbath day, as was his custom. He
stood up to read, and the scroll of the prophet Isaiah was given to
him. He unrolled the scroll and found the place where it was
written: 'The Spirit of the Lord is upon me, because he has
anointed me to bring good news to the poor. He has sent me to
proclaim release to the captives and recovery of sight to the blind,
to let the oppressed go free, to proclaim the year of the Lord's
favour.' And he rolled up the scroll, gave it back to the attendant,
and sat down. The eyes of all in the synagogue were fixed on him.
Then he began to say to them, 'Today this scripture has been
fulfilled in your hearing.'*

That Jesus had a purpose is beyond any doubt, as is his belief that it
was determined not by his own will but by the will of his heavenly
Father. In fact, the short answer to the question 'What was the
purpose of Jesus?' would be, 'To do what his Father required.' That
perfect prayer of submission, 'Yet not my will, but yours be done'
(Luke 22:42), sums up his life of total dedication. In a perfect unity
of purpose, the Son went about the Father's bidding.

But that purpose can be broken down into specific 'goals'. Jesus
knew what he had come to do, and set about fulfilling it completely.
Those goals, at one and the same time, limited his objectives (within
the divine plan, as it were) and gave them wings—eternal issues,
cosmic issues, were at stake. It's fascinating to see how the particular
and the universal come together in the teaching of Jesus about
precisely what he had come into the world to achieve.

For instance, 'I was sent only to the lost sheep of the house of
Israel' (Matthew 15:24). That could be seen as severely limiting the
ministry of Jesus, and indeed, when approached by a Gentile woman

who sought healing for her daughter, he gave this as a reason for declining to get involved. However, when she persisted, and placed herself in a position of very humble dependence, he granted her request, commending her 'great faith' (Matthew 15:21–28). So the 'limitation' was not absolute, as was also shown in his ministry to a Roman centurion whose servant was ill. Yet it did give focus to his mission. The good news of the kingdom was first of all for the people of the covenant, the Jews, and only later for 'all nations' (Matthew 28:19). That was the purpose of God, and Jesus faithfully pursued it.

Jesus said that he came to make a difference, to disturb the present order of things, to 'set a man against his father' (Matthew 10:35). This 'disruptive' element in the teaching of Jesus is often overlooked. He was a radical who challenged, root and branch, many of the most cherished traditions of his hearers. The impact of Jesus on people and their relationships was often, in his own words, to bring 'not peace, but a sword' (Matthew 10:34).

Yet there is also a gentleness in the purpose of Jesus, especially for those who were aware of their need. He hadn't come for the healthy, but for those who knew they were 'sick'. 'Those who are well have no need of a physician', he told the scribes and Pharisees, 'but those who are sick. I have come to call not the righteous but sinners to repentance' (Luke 5:31, 32). We can see that 'gentleness' in his ministry of healing, when he was moved by the plight of the widow at Nain who had lost her only son (Luke 7:11–13) or by the syna-gogue ruler, Jairus, whose little daughter was at the point of death (Luke 8:41). We can hear it in his words of invitation to the 'weary and heavy-laden': 'Come to me... and I will give you rest' (Matthew 11:28).

Perhaps above any other single purpose, Jesus came to proclaim the kingdom of God. Right at the start of his ministry he set out his 'manifesto', as it were. 'Jesus came to Galilee, proclaiming the good news of God, and saying, "The time is fulfilled, and the kingdom of God has come near; repent and believe in the good news"' (Mark 1:14–15). It was the 'kingdom' that *was* the good news, and he had come not only to announce it, but in himself to personify it. By his own obedience to the Father he demonstrated what the life of the kingdom would be like: a life lived in perfect harmony with the love, justice and goodness of God.

In line with that kingdom manifesto was his fulfilment of the messianic prophecy set out at the head of this chapter. Reading these words in his home synagogue at Nazareth, and then announcing their 'fulfilment', was to set out an agenda of liberation—from poverty, from captivity, from blindness, from oppression. In his own life he set people free from some of those kinds of bondage literally, but in his wider purpose he pointed to their spiritual fulfilment as well. He had come into the world to release people from the most crippling slavery of all, to self and sin—a slavery that frustrates the very purpose of God for people made in his own image. Jesus would be the divine catalyst, the cosmic liberator, the 'man of jubilee' who would 'proclaim the year of the Lord's favour', when debts would be cancelled and slaves set free.

That was the divine manifesto. The method of its fulfilment was both simple and profound. 'The Son of Man came to seek out and to save the lost' (Luke 19:10). What Jesus did for three years among the hills of Galilee and in the streets of Jerusalem he still does, because that is the heart of his purpose. He is looking for the 'lost': the valuable thing that is disconnected from its proper place, the 'sheep' that has wandered into trouble, the people who are 'harassed and helpless' (Matthew 9:36). In that sense, we are all 'lost' without God, drifting around in a world we can't understand, trying to find meaning and purpose in it all. It is wonderful to know that the 'Son of Man' who is also the Son of God came specifically to find us and set us on the road to true fulfilment.

To REFLECT

The purpose of Jesus was entirely for the blessing of others. Not one aspect of his purpose was to please himself. Yet as we listen to his teaching and observe his life, we see a man at peace with himself, with his Father and with the world. Is there a clue there to the true path to personal fulfilment?

Other passages you may wish to consult: John 6:38–40; John 17:1–5; John 18:37

PAUSE *for* PRAYER

MATTHEW 28:19, 20

*Go... and make disciples of all nations, baptizing them in the
name of the Father and of the Son and of the Holy Spirit, and
teaching them to obey everything that I have commanded you. And
remember, I am with you always, to the end of the age.*

All the Gospel accounts of the resurrection, except Luke's, refer to a
meeting which the risen Jesus was to have with his disciples in
Galilee. This is Matthew's story, the gathering of the eleven at the
'mountain to which Jesus had directed them'. The purpose of the
meeting quickly becomes clear. The mission of Jesus is not over—far
from it. But from now on it is in their tender hands!

'Go... make disciples... teach them to obey everything that I have
commanded you.' They were now the sole repositories of the message
of Jesus, the very message we have been studying over the last few
weeks. They carried his words in their hearts. They had seen the
miracles, some of them had watched him die, all had now seen the
risen Lord. This was 'good news' for 'all the nations'—the whole
world—and it was their responsibility to pass it on, to bring others to
'sit at his feet' and learn from him.

As we have looked again over these past weeks at the teaching of
Jesus, we may have felt a sense of gratitude, even awe, at the majesty
and authority of his words. But now he asks for more: a real commitment to sharing them with others. 'Go, make disciples, baptize,
teach.'

A PRAYER

*Teacher and Master, write your words on my heart, so that I may
pass them on to others in all their richness.*

MATERIAL for GROUP DISCUSSION

For groups wanting to base a weekly study or discussion on this book, these are suggestions for its use in that way. As a general principle, it's obviously best if all the members of the group read the whole book, if they're to get anything like a complete picture of the teaching of Jesus. So the first twenty minutes or so of the weekly meeting could profitably be spent (perhaps over a cup of tea or coffee) getting feedback from members on the week's readings: problems, insights, reflections, new ideas that they may have experienced. What follows is a list of suggestions (no more than that) for a single topic discussion based on just *one* topic from each week, though incorporating some of the other material. I'm not suggesting that any group would use all of the questions and topics I've given. The leader needs to decide which topics are likely to be most effective discussion starters for his or her particular group.

I've based the material on six topics drawn from the chapters of this book. They are the six topics which, out of all the ones dealt with here, seem to take priority in the teaching of Jesus. At any rate, they are the ones to which the Gospel writers give the greatest emphasis. So in discussing them, and perhaps drawing in elements from the other chapters that have been read during the week by the members of the group, it is fairly safe to say that you are dealing with the heart of the teaching of Jesus.

Week One: Faith and trust (chapter 6), plus Anxiety (chapter 2)

What are the main anxieties that afflict us? (It might be an idea to draw up a list!) How do these anxieties compare with the ones Jesus listed in Matthew 6? And what about anxiety about the future: what might happen, but probably won't?

When people worry, it's not much use saying 'Don't worry' to them! But what, in the light of the teaching of Jesus, can we say? Would it seem impractical, or falsely pious, to ask people to 'have faith in God'? And what exactly would we mean by that?

It might be an idea to draw up a list of ways in which we might define 'faith', as Jesus talked about it. (The list might include things like trust, confidence, belief in God's purposes, and so on.) Why was the Roman centurion such a good example of 'faith'?

What would you say to someone who said that faith was believing the impossible? (Bear in mind that saying of Jesus quoted in each of the synoptic Gospels—see Mark 10:27.)

What can we do to align our faith with God's purpose? It would seem that that's the clue to a life of faith, as Jesus saw it, but, for most of us, *discovering* God's purpose is the difficult bit. Perhaps members of the group could share any personal experience that would throw light on this dilemma.

Week Two: Honesty (chapter 11) and Hypocrisy (chapter 13)

It might be an idea to start by inviting people to comment on the whole principle of absolute honesty. Do they expect other people to tell them the truth (the *whole* truth)? What about so-called 'white lies'? What about putting the best gloss on something, say, a terminal illness, or a business problem?

Then, the group might like to think about honesty in public life. Do we expect politicians and the media to tell us 'the truth', or have we become accustomed to 'management' of the facts to the extent that we don't believe anything we're told? Should a Christian politician always tell all of the truth, even if it would damage his party's chances or undermine a colleague's position?

Do you agree that there's a bit of the hypocrite in all of us? That we all do a bit of 'play-acting' from time to time? Are religious people— even Christians—worse than other people in this respect? And is it worse to fool ourselves than to fool other people?

Do you agree that many people are put off Christianity because they think that some (even many) Christians are insincere? Do you think that such ideas are largely the product of soap-opera images of

'Christians' and even clergy? Is there anything ordinary Christians can do to correct the impression?

'Honesty is the best policy' or 'Truth is its own reward'? What is the best possible motivation for telling the truth and living a truthful life? And should we be influenced by the warning of Jesus that in the end everything will be revealed, even the things we've tried so hard to keep hidden?

Week Three: Kingdom of heaven (chapter 16) and Justice (chapter 15)

As the 'kingdom' is such a vital element of the teaching of Jesus, it might be an idea to invite the group to draw up a list of what seem to be its main characteristics. It might be worth listing them under categories, like 'Whose kingdom?', 'How do you enter it?', 'What are its hallmarks?', 'Differences between the kingdom of heaven and the kingdoms of the world', and so on.

There are many parables of the kingdom, mostly beginning with a phrase such as 'The kingdom of heaven is like…' Again, it might be useful to see how many of those parables members of the group can recall, and what they think each one tells them about the kingdom of heaven.

God's kingdom is the place where he 'reigns', and where his perfect justice applies. If justice is a mark of the kingdom, how could Christians (the people of the kingdom) show their commitment to that justice in our society and in the world?

If the people of the kingdom are all those who have submitted to his rule and are trying to carry out his purpose, do you think that the Kingdom of heaven on earth is just the Church, or more than that? For instance, do you think that God-fearing people who are not 'signed-up' Christians might be part of his kingdom? (This is a difficult question, but it raises very interesting and important questions about God's purpose for those who sincerely believe in him but not in Jesus Christ—for instance, devout Jews and Muslims. Can they be part of his kingdom, while obviously not yet being part of his Church?)

We are told to pray 'Your kingdom come'. What do we think we mean when we pray it? Is this a prayer about the future, or the present? And does it hold those who pray it to any particular commitment? Is the kingdom, in other words, only something for the future, or can we begin to experience its blessings here and now?

Perhaps the group would like to draw up a 'manifesto' for the kingdom of God, setting out its 'programme' and what it stands for. It might even be hung up in church!

Week Four: Priorities (chapter 25) and Purpose of life (chapter 26)

Jesus taught a great deal about priorities, about what really mattered, and what was in the end of secondary importance. It might be an idea to draw up two lists, one of the 'absolute priorities', as Jesus saw them; and the other of the 'secondary things', which the world values enormously but the people of the kingdom should recognize as of passing value. When you've drawn them up, it might be worth discussing how on earth we could commend the priorities of Jesus to a consumer society!

Do you feel that Jesus' teaching about things like money, clothes, food and so on is a bit impractical? And how would you answer that objection, from his own teaching?

'Knowing God' is an elusive idea, yet it seems to be the chief goal of life! How would we describe what it means to us?

How do the priorities of Jesus (his 'programme', as it were) compare with the priorities of your own church (its 'programme')? How can our church life witness to his priorities?

It might be an idea to end the session by drawing up a chart (perhaps for display in church?) setting out what the group sees as the clear priorities of the teaching of Jesus, both for the individual and for the company of his followers.

Week Five: Righteousness (chapter 29) and Sin (chapter 33)

Here are the opposites in the teaching of Jesus, brought together! It might be an idea to start by asking the group to suggest what 'righteousness' means to them—how they would recognize it in someone else, or what goals it sets before them in their own lives.

Jesus taught that righteousness was 'doing what God requires'. To be very practical, how can we know what God requires in particular circumstances? Perhaps members of the group could offer ideas from their own experience of times when they have been led to discover what God required of them.

'Not only the letter but the spirit of the law'—that's a difficult idea. Could the group provide examples of when it would be possible to keep the letter of the law but act against its spirit—and possibly vice versa.

The whole business of evil in a world created by a good God is also a very difficult one. The parable at the head of chapter 29 offers, by way of explanation, a story. It's worth examining it (you can find it in Matthew 13:24–30) to see what we can learn from it both of the origin of evil in the creation, and of God's long-term plan to deal with it. In practice, in everyday experience, what does it mean for the 'good seed' of righteousness and the 'weeds' of evil to be left to grow together? Why would the 'wheat' be in danger if the 'weeds' were to be pulled up, and what does that mean for us?

People outside the Church often complain that Christians are 'always going on about sin' (not that one can recognize the charge in practice!) Still, it might be a good idea for the group to set out, perhaps on a large sheet of paper, what they think 'sin' is, in terms those non-Christians could understand. Is 'lost' a better word than 'sinner' to describe those who have slipped their moral moorings? Should we be afraid of the word 'sin'?

Week Six: His identity (chapter 36) and His purpose (chapter 40)

These subjects should provide an appropriate end to your discussions, because there's no doubt that it is *who Jesus is* and *what he came to do* that determine what weight we give to his teachings.

'Who do you think I am?' was the question Jesus put to his disciples. If he were to put it to you today, what would your answer be? It might help to list on a sheet of paper the answers of the people in the group.

It's obvious that the disciples came fairly slowly, and in some cases painfully, to a full realization of the identity of Jesus. That mirrors the experience of most Christians. Why not spend a quarter of an hour or so inviting members of the group to share their own 'faith journey', being very honest about where they are on it now, and concentrating on our understanding of who Jesus is for us.

The teaching of Jesus was sometimes disruptive: it challenged, disturbed, even angered people, and it divided between those who accepted it and those who rejected it. What does that tell us about the likely impact of the teaching of Jesus when modern people are faced with it in all its bluntness? Is there a danger in presenting an 'acceptable' Jesus?

Then it might help to set out yet another 'manifesto'—this time, the manifesto of Jesus—his 'programme', if you like. What did he come into the world to do? And how did he achieve it?

Finally, to end your studies, why not each share with the group one thing about the marvellous teaching of Jesus that has come to you in a new way during these weeks, and one way in which you intend to apply that teaching in your own life in future.